The Radical Self

University of Missouri Press
Columbia, 1988

The Radical Self

Metamorphosis to Animal Form
in Modern Latin American Narrative

Nancy Gray Díaz

Copyright © 1988 by
The Curators of the University of Missouri
University of Missouri Press, Columbia, Missouri 65211
Printed and bound in the United States of America
All rights reserved

Library of Congress Cataloging-in-Publication Data

Díaz, Nancy Gray, 1942–
  The radical self : metamorphosis to animal form in modern Latin American narrative / Nancy Gray Díaz.
  p. cm.
  Bibliography: p.
  Includes index.
  ISBN 0-8262-0692-1 (alk. paper)
  1. Latin American fiction—20th century—History and criticism. 2. Metamorphosis in literature. I. Title.
PQ7082.N7D48 1988
863—dc19 88-10000 CIP

∞™ This paper meets the minimum requirements of
the American National Standard for Permanence of Paper
for Printed Library Materials, Z39.48, 1984.

To Luis Alberto and
Luis David Díaz
and to my mother,
Jean Selman Gray
and my father,
Earl Wayne Gray

Preface

This essay approaches modern Latin American narrative from a predominantly phenomenological and existential perspective and therefore marks a departure from the main currents of contemporary Latin American criticism, which are sociological, historical, semiotic, feminist, even deconstructionist. Although several of Latin America's most prominent writers and critics have alluded to a tendency to ontological inquiry as an essential ingredient of Magic Realist writing, very little critical attention has been paid to this element. The prevalence of the theme of metamorphosis to animal form provides a significant and immensely valuable key to the revelation of this fundamental aspect of modern Latin American narrative because, as Harold Skulsky has ably demonstrated in *Metamorphosis: The Mind in Exile*, metamorphosis in serious literature inevitably raises questions about what it is to be human. The investigation of the literary treatment of metamorphosis in major texts enables us to uncover problems involving the ontology of human-ness (and also, incidentally, of language and literature) as they are posed in these texts. Nevertheless, the method applied in this essay is not intended to exclude or deny other critical approaches; indeed it borrows from other critical modes whenever helpful. The phenomenological orientation here serves to underscore the richness and originality of Latin American texts by focusing on an important dimension hitherto largely unexplored.

This essay is the culmination of a project that I undertook several years ago in graduate school. While immersed in reading Latin American novels and stories for a special examination topic in the Department of Comparative Literature at Rutgers University, I was struck by the ubiquitousness and variety of animal imagery present in a wide range of texts. Writers belonging to the Realist and Naturalist tradition, such as Mariano Azuela (*Los de abajo*), Alcides Arguedas (*Raza de bronce*), Juan Bosch (*La mañosa*), Ricardo Güiraldes (*Don Segundo Sombra*), José Eustacio Rivera (*La voragine*), and Rómulo Gallegos (*Doña Bárbara*), depict everyday human interaction with the animal world, the pervasive influence of animal behavior in human life, and the way in which animals are perceived to symbolize some aspect of human fate. Rafael Arévalo Martínez (*El hombre que parecía un caballo*) and Mario Vargas Llosa (*La ciudad y los perros*) use metaphorical animal masks for human characters, thereby covering and dis-covering clues to behavior and being. Graciliano Ramos (*Vidas secas*) explores the psyche of a dog. Horacio Quiroga (*Cuentos de amor, de locura, y de muerte*) and Lydia Cabrera (*Cuentos negros de Cuba*) personify animals and make them protagonists. Juan José Arreola and Julio Cortázar revive the bestiary, the former satirizing the moral and aesthetic judgments that we make about beasts (and that tell more about us than about them) and the latter demonstrating how the beast and beastliness invade our psyches. And Borges (*El libro de seres imaginarios*) pays tribute to the power and range of human imagination by gathering together an amazing and amusing collection of beasts of human invention. All of these devices are employed to explore the human by reference to the natural world. Nevertheless, the episodes of metamorphosis that I encountered seemed to me to point more directly than did other modes of animal imagery to the existential basis for the preoccupation with animals.

I have selected for close analysis those texts that I consider to be the most significant historically and the most important theoretically: Alejo Carpentier's *El reino de este mundo*, Miguel Angel Asturias' *Hombres de maíz*, Mário de Andrade's *Macunaíma*, Julio Cortázar's "Axolotl," and Carlos Fuentes' *Zona sagrada*. However, also rich in possibilities for intensive examination are the following: from Spanish America, Horacio Quiroga's "Juan Darién," Demetrio Aguilera-Malta's *Siete lunas y siete serpientes*, Luisa Valenzuela's *El gato eficaz*; from the French Caribbean, *La Bête de Musseau* by Philippe Thoby-Marcelin and Pierre Marcelin, or very important, Simone Schwarz-Bart's *Pluie et vent sur Télumée Miracle* and *Ti-Jean, L'horizon*; and from U.S. Hispanic writing, Rudolfo Anaya's *Bless Me, Ultima*.

A version of chapter 2, "Metamorphosis as Integration: Asturias' *Hombres de maíz*" will soon be published by the *Revista Canadiense de Estudios Hispánicos*, and the editors have graciously granted permission for its inclusion here.

This essay is an outgrowth of my doctoral dissertation, and I expressed in the dissertation the deep gratitude I feel to those scholars and teachers who lent support and guidance to my research. Here I would like to thank my friends and family for their special participation in the development of this project. Diane Marting, Galina DeRoeck, Diann Brown, Joyce Fittipaldi, and Luz María Umpierre have given the kind of spiritual and emotional support that only women who are dear friends and who struggle together can give to each other. My father, Wayne Gray, and my mother, Jean Selman Gray, nourished my love of learning and have given me constant and loving reinforcement in my professional endeavors. My son, Luis David Díaz, is my joy and has given me strength through his good sense and good humor. And I especially and most deeply thank my husband, Luis Alberto Díaz, for his practicality, his unfailing confidence in me, and his devotion.

N. G. D.
November 1987

Contents

Preface, vii

1. Introduction, 1

2. Metamorphosis as Problematic Destiny
   El reino de este mundo, 16

3. Metamorphosis as Integration
   Hombres de maíz, 34

4. Metamorphosis as Cosmic Refuge
   Macunaíma, 51

5. Metamorphosis as Creation Game
   "Axolotl," 72

6. Metamorphosis as Revenge
   Zona sagrada, 83

7. Conclusion, 98

Notes, 103

Bibliography, 115

Index, 123

1 Introduction

When we think of the idea of "form," we may conceive of it as the outward shape of a thing and somehow separate in our minds the shape from the substance. Or, on the other hand, the "form" can be for us the essential determinant principle of the thing, the quality that makes the thing unique. Now let us imagine (as we may have done many times) a human being changing form in some drastic way, taking the shape of a bat, a bird, a shark, a cat, a beetle. What ramifications would such a transformation have on the qualities that are the unique and defining essence of that individual, that self? What, indeed, are those qualities? Many writers of metamorphosis from human to animal form in serious literature have wrestled with the problems of the relation of form to self. In literary metamorphosis the consciousness of the transformed being continues. Yet writers have imagined that it is the most essential self, the root self, the radical self, that is shaken and threatened, extended or divided, with the change of form.

As Harold Skulsky has argued in *Metamorphosis: The Mind in Exile*, metamorphosis in literature involves questions of what it is to be human. He examines conceptions of the human mind and personhood as they are revealed in certain literary metamorphoses and the moral questions that surround transformational crises. "The virtue of fantasy is that some of the intimate features of the terrain of fact can be properly mapped only from the vantage point of the counterfactual."[1] Skulsky shows that in metamorphosis the mind continues as consciousness and remembrance of its own past. In this essay we will be concerned with the ontological problems inevitably posed in serious literature when certain aspects of the self, which were hitherto understood as definitive to one's understanding of the self, are radically altered. Nevertheless, the term *mind* implies a dualism with body (as Skulsky himself admits) that is completely alien to the conception of the self as a totality, and it is this totality, this integrality of the self, menaced as it is by metamorphosis, that emerges as one of the fundamental preoccupations of the literature of metamorphosis.

One purpose of this essay is to propose a method of investigating the very complex phenomenon of metamorphosis in literature that will take into account the existential meanings that surround the phenomenon. The method developed here will analyze the mutability of the world in which the metamorphosis takes place, the mode of being of the transforming character, and the knot of values represented by the metamorphic crisis. This is intended as a method that will facilitate the interpretation of literary metamorphoses wherever they are to be found.

The metamorphosis of a human character to animal form occurs frequently in modern Latin American novels and stories. Often these metamorphoses are climactic events, crucial to the reader's understanding of the character that undergoes transformation and to the meaning of the narrative as a whole. The aims of many modern Latin American writers who depict metamorphoses are both epistemological and ontological; they intend to reveal new ways of perceiving, understanding, and interpreting the world and at the same time to challenge our conception of human being. The second task of this essay will be the interpretation of metamorphoses in five major modern Latin American narratives—*El reino de este mundo* by Alejo Carpentier, *Hombres de maíz* by Miguel Angel Asturias, *Macunaíma* by Mário de Andrade, "Axolotl" by Julio Cortázar, and *Zona sagrada* by Carlos Fuentes.

A number of prominent Latin American writers and critics have made reference to, but have not examined in any systematic way, the ontological questions that Magic Realism engages. Octavio Paz asserts that the urge to metamorphose is fundamental to human being and that the magical art of his contemporaries realizes this desire.[2] Luis Leal states that the principal tendency of Magic Realism is the discovery of the mysterious relationship between man and his "circunstancia."[3] Enrique Anderson Imbert comments that Magic Realism roots itself in being, revealing that being as problematical.[4] Alejo Carpentier explicitly uses the term *ontology* in his formulation of the concept of "lo real maravilloso."[5] And Adalbert Dessau seizes an additional important point as he argues that the roots of Magic Realism are to be discovered in the quest for a genuinely American form of expression that founds itself in ontological inquiry.

Ontológicamente concebida en sus primeras tentativas, esta expresión del "hombre americano", que también había motivado las primeras tentativas del realismo mágico en Carpentier (*Ecué-Yamba-O,* 1933) y Asturias (*Leyendas de Guatemala,* 1930), se libera de su ropaje metafísico original para penetrar en la auténtica vida espiritual de sus protagonistas populares y, sobre todo en la obra de Carpentier, que es la más consecuente en este sentido, en la dialéctica de la historia latinoamericana.

(Ontologically conceived in its first attempts, this expression of "American man," which had also motivated the first attempts at Magic Realism in Carpentier [*Ecué-Yamba-O,* 1933] and Asturias [*Legends of Guatemala,* 1930], frees itself of its original metaphysical dress in order to penetrate the authentic spiritual life of its ordinary protagonists and, above all in the work of Carpentier, which is the most consequential in this sense, in the dialectic of Latin American history.)[6]

The interpretation of metamorphosis from human to animal form facilitates a penetration to the ontological meanings embedded in Magic Realist texts. In the first part of this introduction, then, we will establish the method of investigation, which is derived in large measure from certain principles of existential phenomenology, and in the second part we will explore the issues of metamorphosis as they arise in modern Latin American narrative.

The characteristics of phenomenology that form fundamental guidelines in this essay are (1) the preoccupation with the idea and meaning of self, (2) the focus on the interaction between self and world, (3) the concern with the essential nature of the thing, and (4) the interpretation of the literary image as an intentional object. As Maurice Natanson has written, "Phenomenology and existentialism are efforts to explore man and his existence by placing primary emphasis on the self, understood as consciousness confronting a world and engaged in human action."[7] The phenomenological literary critic focusing on the self may, for example, look at the operations of the consciousness of a protagonist or narrator,[8] the functioning of that self in relation to space or time,[9] or the interaction between text and reader.[10] If phenomenology is a study of essences, it also insists on confronting existence in its presence and immediacy.[11] I see this as the opportunity to strip away temporarily the preconceptions one tends to bring to the text, to seize its immediate impact and to read it closely. At the moments when I confront the phenomenon of literary metamorphosis in the individual text, I describe the narration carefully and plainly. After such a direct encounter with the thing as it is, the critic may build and elaborate an interpretation based on evidence and intuition. The understanding of the image as intentional object means that the image-object is created by an act or acts of consciousness.[12] This view of the literary image distinguishes itself clearly from a psychoanalytical or an archetypal interpretation of the image in that it privileges the conscious over the unconscious in the study of literary creativity. This perspective is then helpful when dealing with images rationally and sequentially elaborated in narrative, and especially in narratives that appropriate the figure of metamorphosis from mythical and folkloric sources in order to adapt it to modern contexts. Nevertheless, the method employed in this essay is finally a synthetic one, based on these phenomenological insights but comparative and with an eye to formal, historical, and generic problems as well.

Metamorphosis: The World, the Self, and the Crisis

The Narrative World

The self, its radical essence and its mode of being, cannot be understood apart from the world that it inhabits. In Martin Heidegger's terms, *Dasein*—

which is defined as "this entity which each of us is himself and which includes inquiring as one of the possibilities of its Being"—has as its most fundamental characteristic "Being-in-the-world."[13] *Dasein*, or the individual self, cannot exist or be imagined to exist outside the context of a world. Furthermore, the contents of one's consciousness are inevitably and irremediably constructed of data apprehended in the world. Thus, if we are to investigate the mode of being of the metamorphosed self, it is imperative to understand the modes of mutability that operate in, and form the structure of, the world that sustains the existence and fills the consciousness of that self.

Metamorphosis is a phenomenon to be examined within another phenomenon, the narrative. The novel or story creates its own world in words, in rhetorical devices, in narrated events, and in symbols. Metamorphosis as literary event transcends plot, however, and informs all levels of meaning in the narrative. As I shall demonstrate, it is integral to the polyphonic structure of the narrative. It is involved in value systems and also may be relevant to anthropological, ethical, social, and psychological, as well as existential, concerns. As it happens, a narrative world in which a metamorphosis can take place is usually highly unstable and dynamic, a world characterized by unpredictable and unsettling mutability.

The "world" of the narrative will be defined as both the depicted fictional environment that surrounds the being to be transformed and also the structure of the narrative, including the language, the rhetorical devices, the pattern of events, the characters, the narrative point of view, all of which unite to become the meaning. That is, the concept of narrative "world" comprehends both content and form, for as Lévi-Strauss reminds us, ". . . la structure n'a pas de contenu: elle est le contenu même, apprehendé [sic] dans une organisation logique conçue comme propriété du réel" (structure does not have form: it is the content itself, apprehended in a logical organization conceived as characteristic of the real).[14] The definition of *mutability* comes from one of the original characterizations of Baroque art by Heinrich Wölfflin: "the apprehension of the world as a shifting semblance."[15] Translating Wölfflin's definition to the art of narrative, let us say that the "apprehension" has to do with the organizing vision of the narrative world by the reader (whether presented in the text by means of the consciousness of a first-person narrator or by other rhetorical means). Let us refer "shifting" to the types of rhetorical devices and events in a narrative that represent the changing of depicted forms in unexpected and irrational ways. "Semblance" will have to do with that other order of Baroque ethos, the interplay of illusion and reality. Thus, a mutable narrative world will be one in which phenomena are often strangely altered in form and therefore in meaning, in which the line between what is supposed to be real and what is not becomes blurred, and in which the reader may be asked to question his or her own sense of stability and stasis in the objective world. (For unlike the fantastic narratives described by Tzvetan Todorov, the Latin American narratives that we will consider assume a vital political and historical relationship between the configurations of the narrative world and those of the external world.)[16]

Metamorphosis

The Self

If we are to speak of metamorphosis in terms of its effects on the self, we must begin with a concept of "self." The self encompasses, first, the unique spatio-temporal history of the individual. Second, the self is able to reflect on its own being. Third, the self is a unity that is capable of contradictions. We will see that in the conventional literary metamorphosis the unique history and memory of the individual survives. (A metamorphosis in which the consciousness passes out of existence must be a metaphor of death.) That is to say, the individual does not become the Other absolutely but rather takes on certain extraordinary characteristics of that Other. Special attention will be directed in this study to the question of the choice of the particular animal mode of being that the writer adopts for the metamorphosis. A character in narrative that is viewed strictly objectively with no reference to its subjective states (either through monologue, dialogue, reported interior monologue, or emblems of feeling and attitude) may be said not to have a self. Certain Ovidian metamorphoses obliterate the possibility of reflection in the character—and this includes some animal metamorphoses as well as transformations into plants and rocks—whereas metamorphoses like that of Gregor Samsa seem to enhance the character's self-awareness. Other literary metamorphoses, like that of Apuleius' Lucius in *The Golden Ass*, are neutral in this respect, for Lucius' powers of consciousness remain unchanged. The examination of metamorphosis in terms of its effect on mind is unsatisfactory because mind does not finally constitute personhood. Paul Ricoeur, among others, has pointed to the distortion of our understanding of the self that is fostered by mind/body dualism and to the need to effect a reconciliation in our thinking between the voluntary (conscious) self and the involuntary (bodily) self in order to apprehend the existential reality of a whole and integrated self.

The nexus of the voluntary and the involuntary does not lie at the boundary of two universes of discourse, one of which would be reflection concerning thought and the other concerning the physical aspects of the body; Cogito's intuition is the intuition of a body conjoined to a willing which submits to it and governs it. It is the meaning of the body as a source of motives, as a cluster of capacities, and even as necessary nature.[17]

Henry Johnstone has explicated the self as a unity that comprehends contradictions, but his point of departure is a contrast between computers and persons.

One and the same person can both know what he is to do and take the blame for not doing it. Persons are unified in a way in which machines are not. . . .
. . . The two concepts of person and contradiction are related in the indissolubly circular way that in philosophy is sometimes characterized as dialectical. Each presupposes the other.[18]

For Johnstone the notion of the self arises out of the difficulty of conceiving a unity that comprises contradictions, paradoxes, and ambiguities. These contradictions, which belong primordially to the self, are one of literature's most treasured themes, and the variety of techniques for exploring them is vast. Let us, however, take note of the differences in modality between three such techniques. In the Euripidean soliloquy (of Phaedra, for example, or Medea), adapted by Ovid to his epic (Medea, again, or Byblis), the character speaks plausibly to herself of that which she wishes and at the same time does not wish; she describes comprehensible emotion and weighs alternatives. In doubling, as for example in Dostoevsky's *The Double,* the self is depicted literally as split, which may be a pathological condition for the protagonist, Goliadkin, but it also symbolizes for the reader the potential for opposite tendencies and impulses in the same self. In metamorphosis, plausibility has again been discarded, and there is no split. Rather, the being undergoes profound bodily change, and the writer elaborates the subjective and objective ramifications to the whole self of that particular kind of reorientation. In all of these, contradiction has become conflict, but the conflict is not necessarily with the external world, as Irving Massey in his study of metamorphosis assumes;[19] it may very well entail a heightening of the contradictions that are the self.

In an examination of metamorphosis and its effect on the self, then, it is appropriate to begin with an analysis of the bodily changes, the way they are conveyed and their metaphorical significance. We will proceed to questions concerning changes in perception, for these lead to alterations in judgment and ultimately in self-reflection. Next, we will consider how metamorphosis affects the individual's voluntary action, his new method of adapting himself to the world or the world to himself. Finally, his relation to time in his altered state will be explicated.

Introduction

The Body

The body is the intermediary by which consciousness expresses its existence in relation to the world. "The body is the vehicle of being in the world, and having a body is, for a living creature, to be interinvolved in a definite environment, to identify oneself with certain projects and be continually committed to them."[20] Thus, the body is very far from being simply form or objective mechanism. It is the vehicle by which the self occupies space and lives time. It is the source of motility, the place where perception and expression occur and the primary creator of meaning.[21]

To the thoughtful and imaginative writer, vital physical change, transform-ation, is going to precipitate or accompany alterations in the self's most basic orientations to its world. In voluntary metamorphoses it is appropriate to ask what problems for the self have arisen from the original human form.

It is in the elaboration of body as function that the body begins to take on existential meaning, but body must also be read in literature as sign, metaphor, or symbol. Thus, in Kafka's tale of metamorphosis, before we begin to recognize the profound social and existential difficulties brought on by Gregor Samsa's transformation, we are struck by the symbolic force of the image of the insect. This is the image of a creature for which we feel no sympathy, no companionship, certainly no admiration, and which is of no use to us; it is ugly, bothersome, and disgusting if worthy of our notice at all. Thus, in order to expose the full meaning of the change of body we must penetrate both its existential ramifications and its symbolic values.

Perception

The concept of perception comprehends, first of all, sense impressions: the visual, tactile, olfactory, auditory, and gustatory faculties by which we inculcate the stimuli of the world. Body, as we noted, is objective sign, but when we speak of perception and the way it is communicated in literature, we have reached a purely subjective realm. A person can understand to a limited degree by analogy the manner in which another human being sees or otherwise perceives an object, but we understand much less well how an animal does so. Here is a whale with one small eye on either side of its head, or a dog which can smell odors and hear sounds that we do not detect. Here is a fly with eyes that are enormous in proportion to the size of its body, or bats which "see" in the dark.[22] And how does it feel to perceive with antennae? Imagining what these kinds of animal sensations must be like belongs to the province of literature, and writers of metamorphosis often try to express for us how it would be to have one's sensations profoundly altered.

Second, once the sense organs are altered, what then become of the affective life and of judgment? Clearly, the value we attach to phenomena is motivated partially by the way they look and feel to us, the way we have accustomed ourselves to classifying them, and the utility that they have for us. This subjective experience of perceptual change is only vaguely suggested in Ovid's external and objectified descriptions of metamorphosis. Indeed, even a character who has undergone metamorphosis and returned to human shape, Macareus (one of Ulysses' men, transformed into a pig by Circe), describes only the outward changes and nothing of how it felt. Nevertheless, we see extraordinary expressions of these imagined states in modern texts. The concept of perception in its ultimate stage has to do with the self's cognition, consciousness, and understanding of itself. If one's body is drastically altered, if one's manner of receiving stimuli is therefore changed, if one's relationships to the phenomena of the world are then transformed, what happens to one's whole conception of self? It is instructive to note in the case of Lucius in *The Golden Ass* that his metamorphosis does not entail changes in sense perception: he preserves his taste for human food to the amazement and glee of his masters. Nevertheless, his ethical judgments and spiritual state, his view of himself and of his place in the world, acquire depth and richness as a result of living as an ass. On the other hand, we would expect to find, and do find (in Kafka's *Die Verwandlung*, for example), metamorphoses that result in a blunting of perceptions, suffering, and a fall, spiritual deterioration. Thus, especially in texts dating from Romanticism on, the issue of changes in perception and all of the ramifications that derive become special areas of interest and even fascination, and we find extraordinary imaginative elaborations of them.

Will

The study of the voluntary and the involuntary, according to Paul Ricoeur, is the exploration of the human being's "structures or *fundamental possibilities*."[23] When we set out to analyze questions relating to the will in a literary text, we direct our attention to actions—how they are carried out and what leads to their conception. We must first consider motivations—needs and desires, both stated and implied. We then can look at the action itself. Finally we must analyze determining factors that might limit the character's capacity to act as he/she might desire.[24] In tales of metamorphosis the mode of acting, the will, the "fundamental possibilities," might be expected to change just as drastically as the body and perception, for movement is carried through by the body, and perception provides its stimulus. We may look also for signs of change in instinctual patterns and habits.

In his interpretation of Aristotle's *Poetics*, Francis Fergusson makes the following comment on the relation of action to the concept of character:

Just after the definition of tragedy (VI.5) Aristotle tells us that action springs from two "natural causes," character and thought. A man's character disposes him to act in certain ways, but he *actually* acts only in response to the changing circumstances of his life, and it is his thought (or perception) that shows him what to seek and what to avoid in each situation. Thought and character together *make* his actions.[25]

Considered in these terms, metamorphosis, being significantly more than a change in circumstance, would be expected to alter the very character of the fictional personage and to change his/her most habitual and instinctual modes of expression through action.

Time

The issue of time for the self resides in the self's consciousness of its own past and of that of its environment, its own present involvement in the world and its potential for being in the future. Georges Poulet has explicated a wide variety of orientations toward time in literature from Montaigne to Proust, demonstrating a method of focusing on time in the text and showing that the issue of time is fundamental to the understanding of the self's mode of existence.[26] However, the task inherent in the present essay differs from Poulet's aims in that we must endeavor to understand time as it operates in the narrative world and, in addition, time as it is lived by the metamorphic character. We will expect to see a person-become-animal alter its orientation in time since we generally perceive animals to live time in significantly different ways than do humans.[27] Do animals remember? Surely they do, for they acquire skills. In literary metamorphosis, when consciousness survives, memory of the being's past continues, although the values attached to those memories may alter. Indeed, the significance of the past may be swallowed up altogether by preoccupation with present or future. Surely the creature's present-ness will change with transformations of body, perception and capacity for action. Furthermore, since the self's potential for being has altered, its anxieties and hopes for the future should also undergo transformation.

The Metamorphic Crisis

The metamorphic crisis dramatizes, encapsulates, and brings into focus the fundamental values of the individual text. Until now we have dealt with metaphysical and existential questions and have made only tangential reference to social issues and ethical values. The analysis of the transformational crisis requires, first of all, attention to social, historical, psychological, and mythological or folkloric factors as they arise in the individual texts. As we turn to the modern Latin American narratives that are the main subject of this essay, we will find concerns with social forces and conditions that must be taken into consideration in any comprehensive interpretation of existential conflict. We will find that metamorphoses often occur in a manner consonant with indigenous mythologies, and we will investigate the ways in which the individual writers have exploited folkloric sources. In some cases, metamorphoses may symbolize psychological aberrations, and we will explore the nature of the pathology. But beyond these factors, it will be necessary to penetrate to the elemental level of the conflict of self and world, for metamorphosis represents the conjunction of self and world, and it plays out the individual's conflict with, or assumption into, the values of that world. This can be done only after we have understood the relation of effects to causes, the nature of cause, and how change takes place, which is a way of talking about time as process in a narrative world. Now we will want to know why the metamorphosis occurs and what it means. For some reason this individual literary character is not allowed, or does not wish, to live in this world in this form. What is the problem? Is it located in the individual or in the world or in the way the two interact? After the author's depiction of each has been analyzed, it will be possible to reach conclusions as to the significance of the metamorphosis within the complex integrity of the work as a whole.

Metamorphosis and Mutability in the Latin American Context

In an essay on the magical in art and art as magic, Octavio Paz points to the human being's longing to become the Other and to the special part that art plays in relation to this impulse.

Lo específico de la magia consiste en concebir al universo como un todo en el que las partes están unidas por una corriente de secreta simpatía. El todo está animado y cada parte está en comunicación viviente con ese todo. . . . Todo tiene afán de salir de sí mismo y transformarse en su próximo o en su contrario: esta silla puede convertirse en árbol, el árbol en pájaro, el pájaro en muchacha, la muchacha en grano de granada que picotea otro pájaro en palacio persa. El objeto mágico abre ante nosotros su abismo relampagueante: nos invita a cambiar y a ser otros sin dejar de ser nosotros mismos. El interés moderno por el "arte mágico" no expresa una nueva curiosidad estética, sino que tiene raíces bastante más hondas: sabemos que nuestro ser es siempre sed de ser "otro," y que solo seremos nosotros mismos si somos

Introduction

capaces de ser otros. Le pedimos al arte el secreto del cambio y buscamos en toda obra, cualesquiera que sean su época y su estilo, ese poder de metamorfosis que constituye la esencia del acto mágico.

(Magic specifically consists in conceiving of the universe as a totality in which the parts are united by a current of secret sympathy. The whole is animated, and each part is in living communication with that whole. . . . Everything is anxious to get out of itself and to transform itself into something similar or into its opposite: this chair can become a tree, the tree a bird, the bird a girl, the girl a pomegranate seed pecked at by another bird in the Persian palace. The magic object opens before us its lightning abyss: it invites us to change and to be other without leaving off being ourselves. The modern interest in "magic art" does not express a new aesthetic curiosity; rather it has much deeper roots: we know that our being is always the hunger to be "other," and that we will only be ourselves if we are capable of becoming other. We ask from art the secret of the change, and we seek in every work, whatever its epoch or style, that power of metamorphosis that constitutes the essence of the magic act.)[28]

Here Paz signals four regions of intellectual inquiry that arise in the treatment of metamorphosis by Latin American narrators: (1) the boundaries between self and Other and how they may be approached or crossed; (2) the longing for transformation, basic to human being and accompanied by a fear of loss of identity; (3) the role of the writer and of literature with regard to change; and (4) the nature of change as effected in metaphorical language. Paz casts his assertions on metamorphosis in ontological and metaphysical terms in order to direct us to the fundamental preoccupations with the stability of our "selves" and with the longing to transform, preoccupations that are manifested in much modern Latin American writing.

Two of the narratives to be studied in this essay, *El reino de este mundo* and *Hombres de maíz*, dramatize the conflict between self and Other specifically in terms of the confrontation between non-Western subcultures and the forces of colonization. Both Alejo Carpentier and Miguel Angel Asturias, born to and educated in the colonizing culture, strive to transform their vision into that of the African slave or the Indian peasant. These are acts of metamorphosis more radical and more reverent than the ordinary creation of fictional characters because of the writers' commitment to the historical destiny of the peoples involved. And these acts are undertaken with the intent of communicating to Western readers an alien reality in such a way as to transform the reader just as the writer has transformed himself. As Georges Poulet says in his phenomenology of reading:

Whatever I think is a part of my mental world. And yet here I am thinking a thought in me just as though I did not exist. . . . Whenever I read, I mentally pronounce an *I*, and yet the *I* which I pronounce is not myself.[29]

The problem posed by Magic Realism (or *lo real maravilloso*) in general and by Carpentier and Asturias in particular is that there exist in different cultures fundamentally distinct systems of interpreting existential reality; and the challenge is for the system by which we perceive and understand to penetrate and interact with that of the Other.

The pure concept of change and the longing to transform reverberate in the social and aesthetic spheres as well as in the existential. By focusing on the individual in his or her moment of metamorphic crisis, Latin American writers affirm a potential for dramatic and drastic change as part of the human's most fundamental mode of being. This view of human being then carries over into social thought, for if the individual person has this primordial capacity, tendency, and longing for change, then society itself is a charged dynamic force. The ability of the individual members of society to transform themselves becomes the whole society's potential for metamorphosis. Thus, the explorations in the ontological realm practiced by Latin American writers are not a purely metaphysical exercise. They are a fundamental grounding for the historical, anthropological, and social visions that we find so compelling in their works.

In the aesthetic realm the thematization of mutability and metamorphosis constitutes itself in the celebrated "neo-Baroque" mode of modern Latin American writing. As I have suggested in the first part of this Introduction, the neo-Baroque tendencies and the recourse to mutability and metamorphosis are intimately linked, for the creation of a mutable narrative world depends both on the continual narration of episodes of transformation and on stylistic devices that convey the sense of a world unstable and in process. Furthermore, the Baroque obsession with the exchange between illusion and reality comes into being through such rhetorical devices as paradox, ambiguity, and hyberbole and through the creation of elaborate image systems that operate in patterns of repetition and reflection.

Conscious as they are of their public and social role, modern Latin American writers frequently explore that role explicitly or implicitly in their fiction. One aspect of the role is that of the transformer, the one who transforms existential reality into fiction, who transforms the reader's *I* into the fictive *I*, the one who may thereby actually influence transformations of social, economic, political reality. It is no accident that some of the model metamorphic figures in their fiction are writers or creators. Mário de Andrade's Macunaíma is the "great transformer" of Indian legend and the inventor of new words. Julio Cortázar's man/axolotl will go home to write of his metamorphic experience. And Carlos Fuentes' Mito, anti-hero of *Zona sagrada*, is myth itself, exposed in constant stages of re-creation. Furthermore, it is not difficult to extend the interpretation to show that the writer/ transformer is the culture hero himself, as we shall see.

The concern with the writer's role leads to what may be an even thornier and more profound inquiry: the questioning of the role of literary language, and especially metaphor, in the expression and transformation of reality. In the prologue to *El reino de este mundo* Carpentier calls into question the purely literary metaphor in his diatribe against Lautréamont, Surrealism, and "lo maravilloso literario."

Pero, a fuerza de querer suscitar lo maravilloso a todo trance, los taumaturgos se hacen burócratas. Invocado por medio de fórmulas consabidas que hacen de ciertas pinturas un monótono baratillo de relojes amelcochados, de maniquíes de costurera, de vagos monumentos fálicos, lo maravilloso se queda en paraguas o langosta o máquina de coser, o lo que sea, sobre una mesa de disección, en el interior de un cuarto triste, en un desierto de rocas.

(But by dint of conjuring the marvelous at whatever risk, the miracle-workers become bureaucrats. Invoked by well-worn formulas that make of certain paintings a monotonous junk shop of melting clocks, of dressmakers' mannequins, of wandering phallic monuments, the marvelous gets stuck in umbrellas or lobsters or sewing machines or whatever, on a dissecting table, in the interior of a sad room, in a desert of rocks.)[30]

In place of the metaphor inspired by dream or the desire for incongruity, Carpentier advocates a mythopoesis founded in marvelous American— which is also for him, historical—reality.

Pero es que muchos se olvidan, con disfrazarse de magos a poco costo, que lo maravilloso comienza a serlo de manera inequívoca cuando surge de una inesperada alteración de la realidad (el milagro), de una revelación privilegiada de la realidad, de una iluminación inhabitual o singularmente favorecedora de las inadvertidas riquezas de la realidad, de una ampliación de las escalas y categorías de la realidad percibidas con particular intensidad en virtud de una exaltación del espíritu que lo conduce a un modo de "estado límite." Para empezar, la sensación de lo maravilloso presupone una fe.

(But many forget, as they disguise themselves as magicians at little cost, that the marvelous begins to be so unequivocally when it arises from an unexpected alteration of reality [the miracle], from a privileged revelation of reality, from an unusual illumination or one singularly favored by the inadvertent richness of reality, from a broadening of the scales and categories of reality perceived with particular intensity by virtue of an exaltation of spirit which leads to a kind of "ultimate state of being." To begin with, the sensation of the marvelous presupposes a faith.)

Y es que, por la virginidad del paisaje, por la formación, por la ontología, por la presencia fáustica del indio y del negro, por la Revelación que constituyó su reciente descubrimiento, por los fecundos mestizajes que propició, América está muy lejos de haber agotado su caudal de mitologías.

(And because of the virginity of its landscapes, its formation, its ontology, the faustian presence of the Indian and the Black, the Revelation that constituted its recent discovery, the fertile cross-breeding that it fostered, America is very far from having exhausted its mythological treasures.)[31]

Transforming fantasy into metaphor is an empty exercise for Carpentier; the task is rather to transform magical and mythical reality into a fiction that interprets that reality as credible and charged with meaning.

Asturias, drawing on Surrealism and what he understands to be the Indian mentality, claims for poetry a somewhat different kind of magical role. Poetry, the magic of the gods, has a sacred function.

La poesía, magia de los dioses, según los mayas y los nahuatles, era el arte de endiosar las cosas. El poeta "endiosa" las cosas que dice y las dice, ni despierto ni dormido, "clarivigilante," es decir, en estado de piedra mágica, de madera mágica, de animal mágico, de fuerza mágica.

(Poetry, magic of the gods, according to the Mayas and the Nahuas, was the art of deifying things. The poet "deifies" the things that he says and he says them neither waking nor asleep, "entranced," that is in the state of magic stone, magic wood, magic animal, magic force.)[32]

Beauty is in nature, but it is poetry that endows beauty with magic, and the mission of poetry is enchantment. This vision of the transformational power of poetic language, of the poetic "act," echoes Octavio Paz's assertion that what we seek in art is the secret of transformation and that the act of metamorphosis effected through the agency of the work of art is its magical essence. However, in Asturias' poetics, and indeed in his Indianist narratives themselves, the difference is that the magical essence has its origins in, and derives its significance from, the alien Indian cultures.

And even Julio Cortázar, in his article, "Para una poética," identifies metaphor as the means by which the human being living in a rational age captures magical affinities comprehended by the "primitive mind."[33] The poet, by means of the magical image, becomes the intermediary between the magician and the philosopher/scientist and carries out the special office of expressing the magic of metamorphosis through metaphor. As we shall see in the necessarily more extended discussion of his theory of metaphor in chapter 5, Cortázar asserts that the metaphor, operating at the ontological level, has to do with the search for, and definition of, being. Its power rests in its ability to overtake and become that which is Other. Cortázar's story "Axolotl" communicates the transition from one state of being to another and the role that art plays with regard to transformation. In his work generally the ontological problem is not posed in terms of non-European cultures, but rather in those of the modern, urbane, rational individual. In "Axolotl" and other Cortázar stories, metamorphosis belongs to the realm of the unconscious and dream, to another reality existing alongside the one we know rationally. The magical powers of metaphor provide the bridge to knowing and crossing over to that other side of being.

The transforming self, that radical self referred to at the beginning of this Introduction, turns out to be, then, the fictional character, the writer, and the reader. Through the analysis of the mutable narrative world and the poetic principles that create it, through the phenomenological investigation of the transformation of the self in depicted metamorphoses, and through the interpretation of the values of the text that are bound up in the metamorphic crisis, we will see revealed a tendency that is vitally important to twentieth-century Latin American literature and intellectual history: the tendency to foster, to explore, and to attempt to capture the possibilities and the powers of change. In the process these writers intend to transform radically themselves, their world, the art of narrative, and us, their readers.

2 Metamorphosis as Problematic Destiny
El Reino de este mundo

Only four years before the appearance of *El reino de este mundo,* Alejo Carpentier published "Los fugitivos," a story in which one of the two protagonists is a dog and the other is a black slave.[1] "Los fugitivos" may be read as an experiment in the exploration of certain aspects of animal being and in the juxtaposition of human and animal responses to similar predicaments, which leads to the treatment of metamorphosis of human to animal in *El reino.* Furthermore, as will be seen in the conclusion to this chapter, the ending of "Los fugitivos" foreshadows in several ways the last sentence of *El reino:* "Arriba, las auras pasaban sobre las ramas, esperando que la jauría se marchara sin concluir el trabajo" (Above, the vultures passed over the branches, hoping that the pack would leave without finishing the job) (*LF,* 137).

The depiction of Perro (literally "Dog," anonymous and prototypical as are many characters in Carpentier's short fiction) alternates between a revelation of subjective states and objective description. The narration of the inner life cannot be classified as reported interior monologue, since the dog does not think in words. Rather, the narrative attempts to capture elemental perceptions and judgments belonging to the dog but related by a distanced narrator in a style characterized by a simplicity of diction unusual in Carpentier's fiction. Perro's primary sense is that of smell, and odors not only make strong impressions on him but also call up strong value judgments. While living in the wild with Cimarrón, for example, the smell of white people becomes detestable and frightening.

Later, when Perro has become one of the wild dogs, the smell of *any* human becomes threatening. Yet, though able to make judgments and decisions and to react acutely to his environment and selected memories, Perro has no emotional life that can be distinguished from a feeling of need. The dialectic between the depicted motivations of the animal and the man can be understood by reference to the distinction between need and desire as described by Paul Ricoeur. Need or appetite "presents itself as an indigence and an exigence, and experienced lack of . . . and an impulse directed toward. . . ." Desire, on the other hand, has as its most important aspect "the anticipation of pleasure which gives the image of the object its full affective nuance and enriches the pure distress of need in a novel way." "Pleasure

Metamorphosis As Problematic Destiny

in fact enters motivation through the imagination."[2] Need in Perro is depicted by Carpentier as an organic function.

Perro tenía hambre. Pero hacia allá olía a hembra. . . . Pero el olor de su propio celo, llamado por el olor de otro celo, se imponía a todo lo demás. Las patas traseras de Perro se espigaron, haciéndole alargar el cuello. Su vientre se hundía, al pie del costillar, en el ritmo de un jadear corto y ansioso.

(Dog was hungry. But over there was a female scent. . . . But the scent of his own heat, aroused by the heat of another, dominated everything else. His back legs stretched forcing his neck to extend. His belly receded into his rib cage in a short, anxious panting.) (*LF,* 118)

The man's motivations, on the other hand, correspond much more often to the image making that Ricoeur associates with desire.

As Perro progresses through the four phases of his life referred to in the story—at the sugar mill, with Cimarrón in the hills, alone in the hills, and as a member of the wild pack—his memory of any aspect of a former phase is called up only by a specific, concrete stimulus. In effect, he becomes aware of the past only when programmed to do so. Several times we are specifically told that he had forgotten his former surroundings. To the extent that he is impelled toward the satisfaction of a need by scent, Perro anticipates in a very limited degree a future, but we are never told that he is even aware of what his goal is. In contrast, Cimarrón vividly remembers the lost pleasures and the horrors of his life as a slave, and after a limited interval of scratching to provide for the immediate future, his thoughts, feelings, and decisions begin to project themselves toward a future routine of dangerous delights (stealing into the sugar mill in search of women and the delicious cooking which he sorely misses).

But that which most severely separates human being and animal being in this story is the consciousness of, and the confrontation with, death. The episode of the carriage accident closely prefigures the end of the story. After the accident, Cimarrón appropriates the priest's cassock, his stole, his money, and the driver's clothing and cuts what must be taken as a comic figure dressed in the cassock and dreaming of erotic pleasures. We note the same playfulness as Perro frolics with Cimarrón's rags after his death. "Perro y la perra gris se divertían como nunca, jugando con la camisa listada de Cimarrón . . . cuando se desprendía una costura, ambos rodaban por el polvo" (Dog and the gray female had more fun than ever, playing with Cimarrón's striped shirt . . . when a seam came apart, they rolled around in the dust) (*LF,* 137). In this parallel we see an essential parity between the animal and the human. However, another parallel episode serves to point up the divergence. One day while living in their cave, Perro uncovers the remains of a human long deceased. "Cimarrón, aterrorizado por la presencia de muertos en su casa, abandonó la caverna esa misma tarde, mascullando oraciones, sin pensar en la lluvia" (Cimarrón, terrified by the presence of the dead in his dwelling, abandoned the cave that same afternoon, mumbling prayers, oblivious to the rain) (*LF,* 124). For Cimarrón, the priest and driver were his oppressors, and he feels no compunction about gaining from their end. But the bones in the cave represent Death, with all of its religious, ritualistic, and premonitory associations, and it is because Perro is unable to conceptualize death, to imagine his own death, to foresee his own future, that he can play innocently with the remains of his former companion. The last line of the story creates the definitive link between the cave episode and the death of Cimarrón. "Durante muchos años, los monteros evitaron de noche, aquel atajo dañado por huesos y cadenas" (For many years the hill people avoided at night that shortcut ruined by bones and chains) (*LF,* 137).

In "Los fugitivos" the destinies of two separate protagonists are recounted in linear fashion, and the dog and man occur both as parallels and antitheses one to the other. In *El reino de este mundo* the slave who is the protagonist, Ti Noel, retains the status of prototype. But in this novella parallels and antitheses fuse as the world becomes startlingly mutable, and the protagonist himself learns to become the animal Other.

Mutability in *El reino* manifests itself in (1) the changes wrought by time in a notably unstable period of Haitian history, (2) the shifts of perspective that create a disorientation in the reader's apprehension of this world, (3) the magical beliefs inherent to Voodoo which inform Ti Noel's and our view of the world, and (4) the Baroque style which constitutes an organic complexity and a naming—which is a re-creation—of the unnamed.

At the end of his prologue to *El reino* Carpentier insists on the historical accuracy of the events and personages in the novella, and Roberto González Echevarría, among others, has meticulously demonstrated the justice of Carpentier's claim.[3] The novella encapsulates approximately sixty years of Haitian history from the 1760s to the 1820s. Part 1 takes place during the colonial period before the French Revolution, part 2 from the beginning of the Bouckman uprising (14 August 1791) to the death of General Leclerc, part 3 during the last years of the reign of Henri Christophe (which lasted from 1811 to 1820) to the night of his death (20 October 1820), and part 4 during the early years of the Republic. It also encompasses the life of Ti Noel, from his young manhood to his death. Each of the first three parts chronicles a popular uprising—the poisonings of domestic animals and of slave owners led by

Mackandal, the Bouckman rebellion, and the revolt against Christophe, respectively. But each uprising leads in turn to new subjugation and repression.[4]

Time functions in *El reino* as a rigidifying process. As the essences of forms continue through time the forms themselves dry out, harden, become sterile and fixed. Often the hardening process is associated with the transformation of the animate and organic to the fixed and immutable quality of artifact, a movement from the "raw" to the "cooked." But the effects of these transformations range from the startling to the horrible and the terrifying. The reader can never view them with complacency.

Our first encounter with this temporal pattern of mutability takes place in the opening chapter when Ti Noel observes wax heads modeling wigs in a barber's window ("Aquellas cabezas parecían tan reales—aunque tan muertas, por la fijeza de los ojos—" [Those heads seemed as real—although their fixed stare was so dead—]) and the heads of dead calves, decorated with parsley, in the butcher's window next door ("cabezas de terneros . . . que tenían la misma calidad cerosa, como adormecidas . . ." [there were calves' heads . . . which possessed the same waxy quality. They seemed asleep . . .]).[5] After the slave rebellion led by Bouckman in part 2, M. Lenormand de Mezy finds the corpse of his second wife frozen in a posture reminiscent of her melodramatic career. In part 3 the blood of bulls decapitated in ritual sacrifice mixes with the cement of the stones of Henri Christophe's fortress, Ciudadela La Ferrière. The king's confessor Cornejo Breille dies by being walled in for having threatened to desert Christophe, thereby becoming "el emparedado," at one, at least linguistically, with the wall. Christophe himself, having been confronted by the ghost of Breille, injured as lightning struck the cathedral, overthrown by the second revolution, and carried away by his fleeing family, dies hearing the drumbeat of the angry Rada gods and is buried in the mortar of his own fortress.

Al fin el cadáver se detuvo, hecho uno con la piedra que lo apresaba. Después de haber escogido su propia muerte, Henri Christophe ignoraría la podredumbre [sic] de su carne, carne confundida con la materia misma de la fortaleza, inscrita dentro de su arquitectura, integrada en su cuerpo haldado de contrafuerte. La Montaña del Gorro del Obispo, toda entera, se había transformado en el mausoleo del primer rey de Haití. (*El reino*, 168)

(Then the corpse came to rest, one with the stone that imprisoned it. Having chosen his own death, Henri Christophe would never know the corruption of his flesh, flesh fused with the very stuff of the fortress, inscribed in its architecture, integrated with its body bristling with flying buttresses. Le Bonnet de l'Evêque, the whole mountain, had become the mausoleum of the first King of Haiti.) (*The Kingdom*, 124)

The character Solimán functions in the story principally to register the shock and horror of the climactic and final encounter with an entity of which "la materia era distinta, pero las formas eran las mismas" (*El reino*, 177) ("the substance was different but the forms were the same"; *The Kingdom*, 133). Years after having been the masseur to Paulina Bonaparte (during her sojourn in Haiti) and knowing intimately the feel of her flesh, he comes upon the marble statue of a naked woman, somehow familiar to him in the Borghese Palace in Rome. He begins to touch, to feel, to knead, but the coldness of the marble immobilizes him in a scream.

Esa estatua, teñida de amarillo por la luz del farol, era el cadáver de Paulina Bonaparte. Un cadáver recién endurecido, recién despojado de pálpito y de mirada, al que tal vez era tiempo todavía de hacer regresar a la vida. Con voz terrible, como si su pecho se desgarrara, el negro comenzó a dar llamadas, grandes llamadas, en la vastedad del Palacio Borghese. (*El reino*, 178)

(This statue, yellow in the light of the lantern, was the corpse of Pauline Bonaparte, a corpse newly stiffened, recently stripped of breath and sight, which perhaps there was still time to bring back to life. With a terrible cry, as though his breast were riven, the Negro began to shout, shout as loud as he could, in the vast silence of the Borghese Palace.) (*The Kingdom*, 133–34)

Driven mad by the transformation, Solimán, in his last appearance in the novella, conjures Papá Legbá to open the way for his return to Dahomey.[6] Even the word itself of Henri Christophe has turned to stone. "El verbo de Henri Christophe se había hecho piedra y ya no habitaba entre nosotros" (*El reino*, 189) ("The word of Henri Christophe had become stone and no longer dwelt among us"; *The Kingdom*, 142).[7]

González Echevarría makes reference to the threat of somatic petrifaction that recurs in Carpentier's work, and he relates this threat to the imposition of meaning and order accomplished by the survival of the past into the present. "If the past as source, as mother, is the realm of formlessness, the past as present is the apotheosis of form, of the father—of archtextuality."[8] However, the interments in stone of Christophe and Paulina are not encountered first as accomplished past; rather we follow these as characters through certain moments of their careers up to their bizarre ends. We see their destinies as process. The metamorphoses of Mackandal and Ti Noel stand as alternatives to death and petrifaction, and an interpretation of the metamorphoses will offer, as well, the key to the understanding of the temporal process that leads to petrifaction.

The second mode in which mutability manifests itself in the world of *El reino* is the shifting of perspective, which renders radically ambiguous any

Metamorphosis as Problematic Destiny

given perception of event or truth. The impersonal narrative voice moves from the consciousness of one character to another in the form of reported interior monologue, and the events and issues of the novella most often come to us filtered through the consciousness of one of the characters, as for example the following:

Monsieur Lenormand de Mezy estaba de pésimo humor desde su última visita al Cabo. El gobernador Blanchelande, monárquico como él, se mostraba muy agriado por las molestas divagaciones de los idiotas utopistas que se apiadaban, en París, del destino de los negros esclavos. ¡Oh! Era muy fácil, en el Café de la Regence, en las arcadas del Palais Royal, soñar con la igualdad de los hombres de todas las razas, entre dos partidas de faraón. A través de vistas de puertos de América, embellecidas por rosas de los vientos y tritones con los carrillos hinchados; a través de los cuadros de mulatas indolentes, de lavanderas desnudas, de siestas en platanales, grabados por Abraham Brunias y exhibidos en Francia entre los versos de DuParny [sic] y la profesión de fe del vicario saboyano, era muy fácil imaginarse a Santo Domingo como el paraíso vegetal de Pablo y Virgina, donde los melones no colgaban de las ramas de los árboles, tan sólo porque hubieron matado a los transeúntes al caer de tan alto. (*El reino*, 83–84)

(M. Lenormand de Mézy had been in a vile humor ever since his last visit to the Cap. Governor Blanchelande, a monarchist like himself, was completely out of patience with the vaporings of those Utopian imbeciles in Paris whose hearts bled for the black slaves. How easy it was to dream of the equality of men of all races between faro hands in the Café de la Régence or under the arcades of the Palais Royal. From views of the harbors of America decorated with compass cards and Tritons with wind-puffed cheeks; from pictures of indolent mulatto girls and naked washerwomen, of siestas under banana trees engraved by Abraham Brunias and exhibited in France along with verses of De Parny and the "Profession of Faith of the Savoyard Vicar," it was very easy to envisage Santo Domingo as the leafy paradise of *Paul and Virginia*, where the melons did not hang from the branches of the trees only because they would have killed the passers-by if they had fallen from such heights.) (*The Kingdom*, 51–52)

Stated or implied, here emerge five views of life in the Antilles: the sentimental vision exemplified by the engravings of Abraham Brunias, the poetry of De Parny, and Bernardin de St. Pierre's novel; the political position of the Jacobins, influenced, as M. Lenormand de Mezy thinks, by the artists; the conservative view of the landowner himself reinforced by that of the colonial governor; the rage of the slaves which has been communicated to us from the beginning of the novella and which we retain mentally as we read this; and our own organizing vision, which takes all of the former views into account as we make our own judgment.

As several critics have observed, a constant dialectic between opposing conceptions of the world provides part of the structural foundation of the narrative.[9] The following is the scene of Mackandal's death and resurrection. We note the contradictory versions of the actual event.

—Mackandal sauvé!
Y fue la confusión y el estruendo. Los guardias se lanzaron, a culatazos, sobre la negrada aullante, que ya no parecía caber entre las casas y trepaba hacia los balcones. Y a tanto llegó el estrépito y la grita y la turbamulta, que muy pocos vieron que Mackandal, agarrado por diez soldados, era metido de cabeza en el fuego, y que una llama crecida por el pelo encendido ahogaba su último grito. Cuando las dotaciones se aplacaron, la hoguera ardía normalmente, como cualquier hoguera de buena leña, y la brisa venida del mar levantaba un buen humo hacia los balcones donde más de una señora desmayada volvía en sí. Ya no había nada que ver.
Aquella tarde los esclavos regresaron a sus haciendas riendo por todo el camino. Mackandal había cumplido su promesa, permaneciendo en el reino de este mundo. Una vez más eran birlados los blancos por los Altos Poderes de la Otra Orilla. (*El reino*, 66–67)

("Macandal saved!"
Pandemonium followed. The guards fell with rifle butts on the howling blacks, who now seemed to overflow the streets, climbing toward the windows. And the noise and screaming and uproar were such that very few saw that Macandal, held by ten soldiers, had been thrust head first into the fire, and that a flame fed by his burning hair had drowned his last cry. When the slaves were restored to order, the fire was burning normally like any fire of good wood, and the breeze blowing from the sea was lifting the smoke toward the windows where more than one lady who had fainted had recovered consciousness. There was no longer anything more to see.
That afternoon the slaves returned to their plantations laughing all the way. Macandal had kept his word, remaining in the Kingdom of this World. Once more the whites had been outwitted by the Mighty Powers of the Other Shore.) (*The Kingdom*, 36–37)

Clearly the last two lines reveal the beliefs of the slaves, but what about the previous paragraph? The expressions "cualquier hoguera de buena leña" and "un buen humo" lend an emotional coloring to the description that one may well attribute to a landowner pleased with his own comfort and content with this satisfactory conclusion to the slave rebellion. In addition, the crispness of "Ya no había nada que ver" may remind us of the reputed succinctness of the landowners' native tongue. Thus, the narrative gives us two alternate views of what has occurred, but what is the reality of the event? Did Mackandal burn or metamorphose? We simply do not know. Whether paradox or ambiguity, this literary event belongs to the realm of the mutable as defined in this essay.

Carpentier states in the prologue that a sense of the marvelous presupposes a faith, and in *El reino* major political and social change comes about through the workings of the gods or of men endowed with god-given

Metamorphosis as Problematic Destiny

powers. Mackandal, who is at the beginning a combination of the Haitian storyteller and the African *griot*,[10] accomplishes the mass poisonings with the help of Maman Loi, who as a *mambo* would have the power of communication with the gods as well as arcane knowledge of sorcery and cures.[11] By chapter 6 of part 1, Mackandal has become an *houngan*, the masculine equivalent of the *mambo* and has been endowed with the power of metamorphosis (*El reino*, 50–51). The words of Bouckman, the Jamaican, make explicit in part 2 what will remain implicit throughout the rest of the story: the earthly events play out a war of the gods.

—El Dios de los blancos ordena el crimen. Nuestros dioses nos piden venganza. Ellos conducirán nuestros brazos y nos darán la asistencia. ¡Rompan la imagen del Dios de los blancos, que tiene sed de nuestras lágrimas; escuchemos en nosotros mismos la llamada de la libertad! (*El reino*, 79)

("The white men's God orders the crime. Our gods demand vengeance from us. They will guide our arms and give us help. Destroy the image of the white man's God who thirsts for our tears; let us listen to the cry of freedom within ourselves.") (*The Kingdom*, 48–49)

And at the end of part 2 after Paulina Bonaparte has left the island wearing an amulet of Papá Legbá, the Loas have triumphed. "Ahora, los Grandes Loas favorecían las armas negras. Ganaban batallas quienes tuvieran dioses guerreros que invocar. Ogún Badagrí [the Voodoo god of war] guiaba las cargas al arma blanca contra las últimas trincheras de la Diosa Razón" (*El reino*, 115) ("Now the Great Loas smiled upon the Negroes' arms. Victory went to those who had warrior gods to invoke. Ogoun Badagri guided the cold steel charges against the last redoubts of the Goddess Reason"; *The Kingdom*, 79–80).

In part 3 the former chef turned king, Henri Christophe, has betrayed the African gods by embracing Christianity and cruelly subjugating their people. On the night of his suicide, the deserted king observes a terrifying disjunction of reality.

El Salón de los Espejos no reflejó más figura que la del rey, hasta el trasmundo de sus cristales más lejanos. Y luego, esos zumbidos, esos roces, esos grillos del artesonado, que nunca se habían escuchado antes, y que ahora, con sus intermitencias y pausas, daban al silencio toda una escala de profundidad. Las velas se derretían lentamente en sus candelabros. Una mariposa nocturna giraba en la sala del consejo. Luego de arrojarse sobre un marco dorado, un insecto caía al suelo, aquí, allá, con el inconfundible golpe de élitros de ciertos escarabajos voladores. . . . El rey se apoyó en la balaustrada, buscando la solidez del mármol. (*El reino*, 156–57)

(The Hall of Mirrors reflected only the figure of the King to the farthest reach of the most remote mirrors. And then, those buzzes, those slitherings, those crickets in the beamed ceilings which had never been heard before, and which now, with their intervals and rests, gave the silence a gamut of depth. The candles were slowly melting in the candelabra. A moth was circling the council room. After hurling itself against a gilded frame, an insect fell to the floor, first here, then there, with the unmistakable whirring of a flying beetle. . . . The King leaned against the balustrade, seeking the solidity of the marble.) (*The Kingdom*, 113-14)

The coming to life of the walls, the bustling of the insects, but especially the appearance of the nocturnal butterfly (or moth) suggest the return and presence of Mackandal, come once again to take his revenge. As has been pointed out, Solimán, another, yet lesser, traitor to his people, meets a similarly horrible end. The deceptive stability of marble has betrayed them both, and the mutability wrought by the Voodoo powers triumphs.

On the other hand, Ti Noel in part 4 has been possessed by the King of Angola,[12] thereby earning the devotion of his neighbors and acquiring his own powers of metamorphosis. He, in turn, calls on the elements, as Bouckman had done, to bring forth calamity on the new subjugators. And the great green wind, its origins in ancient Guinea, does precisely that.

The preceding discussions of the transforming function of time, of ambiguity in perspective, of mutability by the agency of gods and magic, have provided clues toward the defining of Carpentier's own conception and artistic realization of a Baroque aesthetic. As is well known, Carpentier proclaimed that Latin American art was always Baroque, "desde la espléndida escultura precolombina y el de los códices, hasta la mejor novelística actual de América, pasándose por las catedrales y monasterios coloniales de nuestro continente. . . . El legítimo estilo del novelista latinoamericano actual es el barroco" (from the splendid pre-Columbian sculpture and the codices to the best contemporary novel-writing in America, by way of the colonial cathedrals and monasteries of our continent. . . . The legitimate style of the contemporary Latin American novelist is the Baroque).[13] His most eloquent elaboration of his own language-created Baroque world is chapter 24 of *El siglo de las luces*.[14] Here Esteban and the passengers have just left the horror and confusion on Guadelupe. Carpentier describes them as "salidos de una temporalidad desaforada para inscribirse en lo inmutable y eterno" (having just come out of a chaotic temporality in order to inscribe themselves on the immutable and eternal) (*El siglo*, 175). The timelessness of the ocean and the luxury of escape stimulate Esteban to look closely at his surroundings and to reflect. The elemental ocean flora and fauna are linked to the mythical, the primordial, the timeless, the archetypal.

Metamorphosis as Problematic Destiny

La selva de coral hacía perdurar, en medio de una creciente economía de las formas zoológicas, los primeros barroquismos de la Creación, sus primeros lujos y despilfarros: sus tesoros ocultos donde el hombre, para verlos, tendría que remedar el pez que hubiese sido antes de ser esculpido por una matriz, añorando las branquias y la cola que hubieran podido hacerle elegir aquellos paisajes fastuosos por una perenne morada. Esteban veía en las selvas de coral una imagen tangible, una figuración cercana—y tan inaccesible, sin embargo—del Paraíso Perdido, donde los árboles, mal nombrados aún, y con lengua torpe y vacilante por un Hombre-Niño, estarían dotados de la aparente inmortalidad de esta flora suntuosa, de ostensorio, de zarza ardiente, para quien los otoños o primaveras sólo se manifestaban en variaciones de matices o leves traslados de sombras. . . .

(The coral jungle perpetuated, in the middle of an increasing economy of zoological forms, the first Baroquisms of the Creation, its first lushness and prodigality, its hidden treasures where man, in order to see them, would have to imitate the fish that he had been before being sculpted in the womb, longing for the gills and the tail which had made it possible for him to choose these fabulous landscapes for a perennial abode. Esteban saw in the coral jungles a tangible image, a figuration so near—and so inaccessible, nevertheless—of Paradise Lost, where the trees, still misnamed, and with the dull and vacillating language of a Child-Man, would be endowed with the apparent immortality of this sumptuous flora, of the monstrance, of the burning bush, for whom the autumns and springs manifested themselves in variations of shades or trifles brought forth from shadows. . . .) (*El siglo*, 177)

Two pages later Carpentier describes the language and style appropriate to the creation of his particular mythical world.

Esteban se maravillaba al observar cómo el lenguaje, en estas islas, había tenido que usar de la aglutinación, la amalgama verbal y la metáfora, para traducir la ambigüedad formal de cosas que participaban de varias esencias.

(Esteban marvelled as he observed how the language of these isles had had to make use of agglutination, verbal amalgamation, and metaphor to translate the formal ambiguity of things that partook of diverse essences.) (*El siglo*, 179)

The Baroque reality of American nature, which the writer must capture, consists in ever variant amalgamations, essences transforming essences, and those ever suggesting others. The constant re-creation recalls a Genesis, the primordial combining, and the process both calls the writer to his task and becomes the metaphor for that task. Thus, the very diction and syntax of the narrative are for Carpentier a transforming, a naming and a renaming, as González Echevarría points out,[15] a tangling, untangling, and fusing of disjunctive elements. The following description of Ti Noel's musings as he looks at the juxtaposed heads in the windows of barber and

26   The Radical Self

butcher is a complex of images that will become distorted and will recur later in the narrative.

. . . Ti Noel se divertía pensando que, al lado de las cabezas descoloridas de los terneros, se servían cabezas de blancos señores en el mantel de la misma mesa. Así como se adornaba a las aves con sus plumas para presentarlas a los comensales de un banquete, un cocinero experto y bastante ogro habría vestido las testas con sus mejor acondicionadas pelucas. No les faltaba más que una orla de hojas de lechuga o de rábanos abiertos en flor de lis. Por lo demás, los potes de espuma arábiga, las botellas de agua de lavanda y las cajas de polvos de arroz, vecinas de las cazuelas de mondongo y de las bandejas de riñones, completaban, con singulares coincidencias de frascos y recipientes, aquel cuadro de un abominable convite. (*El reino*, 25)

(. . . it amused Ti Noel to think that alongside the pale calves' heads, heads of white men were served on the same tablecloth. Just as fowl for a banquet are adorned with their feathers, so some experienced, macabre cook might have trimmed the heads with their best wigs. All that was lacking was a border of lettuce leaves or radishes cut in the shape of lillies. Moreover, the jars of gum arabic, the bottles of lavender water, the boxes of rice powder, close neighbors to the kettles of tripe and the platters of kidneys, completed, with this coincidence of flasks and cruets, that picture of an abominable feast.) (*The Kingdom*, 4–5)

The image of the calves' heads foreshadows the decapitation of the bulls in part 3, the birds and their feathers anticipate the last image of the novella (only there the bird will have eaten the man), the expert cook will reoccur as Henri Christophe, and the abominable banquet suggests the ritual celebration that will swallow him up. The constant manipulation and re-formation of word-created entities that constitute *El reino de este mundo* realize a narrative world ever renewing itself in a modality of esoteric ec-stasy.

The metamorphoses of the two principal characters of *El reino de este mundo*—Mackandal and Ti Noel—stand both in opposition to and in consonance with the mutable world which is their context. Metamorphosis into animal form clearly contrasts with the pattern of petrifaction outlined above, and indeed, to become an animal in this novella is a positive process because it enables the being to participate in the dynamism that is the essence of life and art in this created world. Nevertheless, metamorphosis finally reveals itself as problematic destiny.

The metamorphoses of Mackandal are a recorded part of the legend of this Haitian hero, and Carpentier has taken the description of his death and transformation from historical sources.[16] Because of his stature as culture hero, as mentor, as model, Mackandal appears more distanced, less ironized, less flawed than Ti Noel can be even at the end of the novella. We are introduced to Mackandal in the first chapter through the thoughts of Ti

Metamorphosis as Problematic Destiny

Noel, and the hero's teachings and actions are nearly always shown in terms of the emotional effects and motivations that they produce in the younger man. The metamorphoses of Mackandal are willed, motivated by rage and a will to action and power, and they realize a transcendance, a liberation from the limitations of human-ness. In his human, temporal existence Mackandal suffers the insult and humiliation of his slavery and also a traumatic injury which necessitates the amputation of his arm. The forms that he takes through metamorphosis recuperate and enhance his freedom and esteem and compensate for his bodily loss.

Todos sabían que la iguana verde, la mariposa nocturna, el perro desconocido, el alcatraz inverosímil, no eran sino simples disfraces. Dotado del poder de transformarse en animal de pezuña, en ave, pez o insecto, Mackandal visitaba contínuamente las haciendas de la Llanura para vigilar a sus fieles y saber si todavía confiaban en su regreso. De metamorfosis en metamorfosis, el manco estaba en todas partes, habiendo recobrado su integridad corpórea al vestir trajes de animales. (*El reino*, 55–56)

(They all knew that the green lizard, the night moth, the strange dog, the incredible gannet, were nothing but disguises. As he had the power to take the shape of hoofed animal, bird, fish, or insect, Macandal continually visited the plantations of the Plaine to watch over his faithful and find out if they still had faith in his return. In one metamorphosis or another, the one-armed was everywhere, having recovered his corporeal integrity in animal guise.) (*The Kingdom*, 28)

Mackandal's powers of vision have been metaphorically telescopic, that is, he has maintained a panoramic vision of his own past and his nation's past and has foreseen a future of freedom and renewal for his people. His vision has been literally microscopic as well, for he has penetrated to the primary properties of individual plants and insects. In finally assuming the shape of the moth, or the insect, he becomes the perception, microscopic in size and yet able to view from above and at a distance the accomplishment of his historic aims. For Mackandal, as for Carpentier in this novella, the kingdom of animals provides a fundamental symbology for action and essence in the kingdom of this world.[17]

Mackandal the human is one of those supremely gifted individuals who are able to conceive imaginative goals and the effective plans of action to carry them out. His metamorphoses are a part of the calculation, a pragmatic choice which allows him to execute his mission to liberate his people and to redress the injustices and shame that they have endured. In addition, these transformations serve as model and inspiration to the slaves and as absolute assurance of the rightness of their cause; not only does the magic of his power impress itself on them but also the pervasiveness of his presumed presence keeps hope and determination alive.

Clearly, the metamorphoses of Mackandal are a transcendance of time and death. He has become part of the other kingdom and at the same time remains manifest in the imaginations of mortals and in occasional animal form. Carpentier is perhaps suggesting by this continual presence that Mackandal has become a *loa* in his own right.[18] Whether or not this is the case, the writer documents in the chronicle of Mackandal the historical process that generates and perpetuates myth.

The metamorphoses of Ti Noel both parallel and ultimately cast a shadow on those of Mackandal. Although we do not know many details of Ti Noel's biography, he is anything but an anonymous character. The narrative radiates with his beliefs, his convictions, his mental images, and the ways in which the impressions of the world work on his consciousness. In many ways the experiences of Ti Noel are meant to typify those of 500,000 black Haitian slaves of this epoch, at least up to the moment of his possession, his metamorphoses, the flash of his existential insight, and his death. These events, which take place in the last three chapters of part 4, turn the narrative around in a heretofore unexpected way by raising Ti Noel to the level not of prototypical Haitian slave of a particular period, but of prototypical human being. In his metamorphoses Ti Noel imitates his lifelong hero but then finds that Mackandal's way will not suit him.

Ti Noel's experiences in animal shapes depict in abbreviated form the view of animal existence that is more fully elaborated in "Los fugitivos." At the end of his life, severely disillusioned by the reemergence of oppression in the form of the mulatto surveyors, Ti Noel decides it might be better to be an animal.

Ya que la vestidura de hombre solía traer tantas calamidades, más valía despojarse de ella por un tiempo, siguiendo los acontecimientos de la Llanura bajo aspectos menos llamativos. Tomada esa decisión, Ti Noel se sorprendió de lo fácil que es transformarse en animal cuando se tienen poderes para ello. (*El reino*, 190)

(Inasmuch as human guise brought with it so many calamities, it would be better to lay it aside for a time, and observe events on the Plaine in some less conspicuous form. Once he had come to this decision, Ti Noel was astonished at how easy it is to turn into an animal when one has the necessary powers.) (*The Kingdom*, 143)

At first he tries a series of transformations into various animal forms, but these experiences occasion only disappointment.

Como prueba se trepó a un árbol, quiso ser ave, y al punto fué ave. Miró a los Agrimensores desde lo alto de una rama, metiendo el pico en la pulpa violada de un caimito. Al día siguiente quiso ser garañon y fué garañon; mas tuvo que huir prestamente de un mulato que le arrojaba lazos para castrarlo con un cuchillo de cocina. Hecho avispa, se hastió pronto de la monótona geometría de las edificaciones de cera. Transformado en hormiga por mala idea suya, fué obligado a llevar cargas enormes, en interminables caminos, bajo la vigilancia de unos cabezotas que demasiado le recordaban los mayorales de Lenormand de Mezy, los guardias de Christophe, los mulatos de ahora. (*El reino*, 190-91)

(In proof of this he climbed a tree, willed himself to become a bird, and instantly was a bird. He watched the Surveyors from the top of a branch, digging his beak into the violated flesh of a medlar. The next day he willed himself to be a stallion, and he was a stallion, but he had to run off as fast as he could from a mulatto who tried to lasso him and geld him with a kitchen knife. He turned himself into a wasp, but he soon tired of the monotonous geometry of wax constructions. He made the mistake of becoming an ant, only to find himself carrying heavy loads over interminable paths under the vigilance of big-headed ants who reminded him unpleasantly of Lenormand de Mézy's overseers, Henri Christophe's guards, and the mulattoes of today.) (*The Kingdom*, 143-44)

In the last chapter, entitled "Agnus Dei," Ti Noel gladly welcomes the migration of geese, a species that he has most especially admired, and Carpentier elaborates more fully the nature of the metamorphic crisis that follows. Ti Noel appreciates the intelligence, the joy of the geese and the absence of authoritarianism in their society. And so he becomes a goose. At first the geese receive him with threatening gestures, and he decides to be discreet and self-effacing. Nevertheless, they treat him with disdain. He tries to win the favor of the females by revealing the hiding place of certain tender roots, but "las colas grises se movían con disgusto, y los ojos amarillos miraban con una altanera desconfianza, que reiteraban los ojos que estaban del otro lado de la cabeza" (*El reino*, 195) ("their gray tails twitched with displeasure and their yellow eyes regarded him with haughty suspicion, repeated by the eyes on the other side of the head"; *The Kingdom*, 147). The clan reveals itself as a community of aristocrats, closed to any outsider. Ti Noel realizes that he can never obtain access to the rites of this group. No goose had danced at his wedding, and none had witnessed his birth.[19]

It is at this point that Ti Noel comprehends that metamorphosis for him is cowardice. He excuses the transformations of Mackandal as expedients consonant with his mission as servant of his people. At the moment in which Ti Noel regains human form he experiences "un supremo instante de lucidez." It is an almost perfect narration of the Heideggerian "moment of vision."[20] Here, in a most startling *tour de force*, Ti Noel does what no character in the novella has been capable of doing: he reflects profoundly on his own being. He relives all that he has been, even to the heritage of his ancient African ancestors. He experiences a cosmic exhaustion and thinks reflectively of what he has inherited (in terms of tradition and culture) and of what he leaves behind. He sees human existence as suffering, as work, as hope, and as disillusionment. But the essential characteristic of the human being is that of imposing upon himself tasks, of striving always to become better than he is. In the Kingdom of Heaven everything is already accomplished.

En el Reino de los Cielos no hay grandeza que conquistar, puesto que allá todo es jerarquía establecida, incógnita despejada, existir sin término, imposibilidad de sacrificio, reposo y deleite. Por ello, agobiado de penas y de Tareas, hermoso dentro de su miseria, capaz de amar en medio de las plagas, el hombre sólo puede hallar su grandeza, su máxima medida en el Reino de este Mundo. (*El reino*, 197)

(In the Kingdom of Heaven there is no grandeur to be won, inasmuch as there all is an established hierarchy, the unknown is revealed, existence is infinite, there is no possibility of sacrifice, all is rest and joy. For this reason, bowed down by suffering and duties, beautiful in the midst of his misery, capable of loving in the face of afflictions and trials, man finds his greatness, his fullest measure, only in the Kingdom of This World.) (*The Kingdom*, 149)

Although Carpentier provides no direct description of Ti Noel's body, one can deduce certain physical characteristics. He has always been capable of hard work and has left "hijos desmemoriados," at least a dozen of them, as we know from an earlier reference. He has had great energy for aggressive rebellion, even in his later years, for he has taken an active part in the sacking of Sans-Souci. Therefore, we can picture him as sturdy, muscular, vigorous. However, the reference to his "cuerpo transcurrido" suggests that he has undergone the natural bodily changes associated with old age. (He is probably near eighty.) In his metamorphoses he seems to regain a more youthful condition. He can flee the mulatto who wants to castrate him, carry heavy loads as an ant, and as a gander of course he courts the females. The rejection of metamorphosis thus results in an acceptance of diminished strength, endurance, and vitality.

From the analysis of the contrast in animal and human modes of perception and judgment in "Los fugitivos," it is clear that Carpentier's animals are devoid of the most significant of Ti Noel's personal qualities, his imagination. Son of a beloved and ancient land that he has never seen, Ti Noel has nevertheless created a whole system of pictures, images, associations, and values that derive from that land and its people. As an exile, he is able to know, retain, and cherish this heritage only through memory and imagination. Although we are not told that he loses these mental capacities when he metamorphoses, the whole purpose of his last transformation is to become a

Metamorphosis as Problematic Destiny 31

participant in a different, more coherent and less complex, society. One assumes that if he were to have become integrated into the goose clan, the richness of his own cultural heritage would eventually have been lost to him.

Perro's killing of Cimarrón illustrates the central problem of metamorphosis in *El reino*. It is not the coldness and immorality (by the standard of human sensibilities) that count; it is rather the mechanical nature of the response. It is not clear why Perro responds to the overseer's order so long after it had been given, but the killing nevertheless manifests itself as reflex. In all of Carpentier's descriptions of animals, the animals behave in ways that appear as set, fixed, and established. Indeed, the slaves had known Mackandal in his animal forms precisely because he behaved in ways uncharacteristic of those species (the moth appeared in daylight, the dog stole his master's meat). Thus, the decision in favor of human being is an affirmation of human freedom to choose. The capacity to metamorphose itself is a powerful instrument of liberation, but once the change is effected, freedom will inevitably diminish.

Metamorphosis, however, enables the individual to transcend time and death. It postpones an absolute end, and allows an indefinite continuation of existence. Ti Noel has become fully disillusioned with the past, seeing his people once again subordinate, and with himself for not being able to put an end to the oppression. Yet in the end, by rejecting metamorphosis, he affirms both his ties to the past and his obligations to the future.

Thus, the metamorphic crisis and its aftermath represent the core of the values of the text, the knot in which are bound up all the strands of theme and meaning. Despite the emphasis on existential issues in *El reino* developed in this essay, however, it is emphatically not my contention here that this is "una novela de tesis, es decir, una novela interesada única y exclusivamente en mostrar el destino del hombre en la tierra" (a thesis novel, that is, a novel interested only and exclusively in showing the destiny of man on earth).[21] Carpentier finds it necessary to develop an ontology and system of existential values as underpinning and support for the social and political positions and interpretations that undeniably occupy a central place in the meaning that is the novella. But how exactly do all of the disparate elements which we have seen relate to each other and what finally do we come to understand from the novella about human existence, one's social role, or time, history, and myth?

The ending of the novella is enigmatic and therefore controversial. The terrible hurricane sweeps the island. "Y desde aquella hora nadie supo más de Ti Noel ni de su casaca verde con puños de encaje salmón, salvo, tal vez, aquel buitre mojado, aprovechador de toda muerte, que esperó el sol con alas abiertas: cruz de plumas que acabó por plegarse y hundir el vuelo en las espesuras de Bois Caimán" (*El reino*, 198) ("From that moment Ti Noel was never seen again, nor his green coat with the salmon lace cuffs, except perhaps by that wet vulture who turns every death to his own benefit and who sat with outspread wings, drying himself in the sun, a cross of feathers which finally folded itself up and flew off into the thick shade of Bois Caíman"; *The Kingdom*, 150). Three possible interpretations suggest themselves: (1) the vulture is Ti Noel, metamorphosed once again; (2) the vulture is purely symbolic; and (3) the vulture is an anonymous bird that has just eaten at the remains of the protagonist. Emma Speratti-Piñero has offered an admirable interpretation of the vulture as the apotheosis of Ti Noel.[22] She points out that once a person has been possessed by a *loa*, he/she has gained the right to immortality, and that Ti Noel survives and returns to the Bois Caiman, flaunting himself as the Baron Samedi's black cross and serving his native land by cleaning it of its corruption. She also provides a refreshing reminder to those who attribute Christian beliefs to Carpentier that his Christian symbology is often mocking and ironic.[23]

In considering this interpretation of the vulture, however, one should recall that Ti Noel has just rejected metamorphosis as appropriate destiny and has affirmed a specifically human mode of being in its materiality as well as in its spiritual essence. As symbol, the vulture of the last sentence of the novella provides a companion figure to the animal image that opens the novella. "Entre los veinte garañones traídos al Cabo Francés por el capitán de barco que andaba de media madrina con un criador normando, Ti Noel había elegido sin vacilación aquel semental cuadralbo, de grupa redonda, bueno para la remonta de yeguas que parían potros cada vez más pequeños" (*El reino*, 23) ("Of the twenty stallions brought to Cap Français by the ship's captain, who had a kind of partnership with a breeder in Normandy, Ti Noel had unhesitatingly picked that stud with the four white feet and rounded crupper which promised good services for mares whose colts were coming smaller each year"; *The Kingdom*, 3). The stallion and vulture represent two points in the cycle of the secular and organic—fertilization and reabsorption into the material fabric that combines and recombines earthly life. In effect, Ti Noel has chosen the natural destiny of human beings, and the vulture, behaving according to its conditioned pattern, has taken advantage in order to fulfill its role in the amalgamation process which is for Carpentier both existential process and aesthetic principle.

As political narrative, Carpentier's novella puts forth a view of revolution as dialectic. The clash between black and white produces the mulatto. The battle between African gods and the European cult of reason and French Catholicism engenders a syncretic religion. Far from being a negative depiction of revolution, the dialectical historical process and Ti Noel's moment of vision reveal collective human existence as struggle, suffering, fulfillment, and challenge. The figures of Christophe and Paulina, on the other hand, reveal comfort and stasis as suffocation, choking both the individuals who seek and impose it and, more important, the others who must be subjugated in order to support it. Petrifaction is both destiny and metaphor, not just for the survival of the past into the present but also for isolation from the community and its collective struggle.

Ti Noel, Little Christmas, whose Christ-like associations have been signaled by several critics,[24] embodies a new beginning. Here the trinity breaks down, for although the gods reign, the son chooses mortality, and the Holy Spirit/dove becomes a vulture. The new Son of Man rejects transcendance and consigns his remains to the earth, the sky, and the water.

Time, then, operates as paradoxical process. Historical time is created out of a chain of cause and effect which is at the same time linear and cyclical. The best of mortals in this narrative world may choose between metamorphosis, a linear transcendance, or mortality, which is death and natural cycle. The choice for Ti Noel and for Carpentier is the eternal recombining. Thus, the faith that Carpentier maintains we must have is more than faith engendered by the veritable myths created in the history of American struggles for liberation; it is also faith in the individual human being's ability to commit the self to its frightful, yet fruitful, final destiny in the Kingdom of this World and to find joy and sacred meaning in that destiny.

3 Metamorphosis as Integration
Hombres de maíz

Like Carpentier in *El reino*, Miguel Angel Asturias informs his novel *Hombres de maíz* with the conceptual and religious perspective of a people who interpret the world in ways radically different from the majority of his readers, who are educated in the European tradition. Indeed, the mythology to which *Hombres de maíz* has reference is integral to the novel to such an extent that the events of the novel are nearly unintelligible without some initiation into that mythology. Furthermore, the structure of the novel, undeciphered by its early critics,[1] becomes apparent only in the light of certain mythological patterns and is of an order of complexity and originality startling even in this century of remarkable literary experimentation. Recourse to anthropology is only part of the answer to the critic's dilemma in trying to discover opaque meanings in Asturias' work, however, for Asturias' penetration into indigenous culture is not, like Carpentier's, primarily intellectual and scholarly, but rather intuitive, visionary, dreamlike. The sources of his creative vision in *Hombres de maíz* and in his other Indian novels, as he tells us in his many interviews,[2] are the memories of contact with Indians during his youth—memories excavated from his unconscious during trancelike periods of automatic writing—and the Maya/Quiché texts on which he carried out his scholarly work at the Sorbonne.

In his book *Hombres de maíz: Unidad y sentido a través de sus símbolos mitológicos*, Emilio F. García has explicated the novel's mythological symbolism, which is based primarily on the *Popol Vuh*. García argues convincingly that Gaspar Ilóm, whose dream, rebellion, and death set in motion the action of the novel, represents Hunahpú, the god of corn. Gaspar's wife, as we learn in the novel, is the rain, and Martín, their baby son, is the corn. At his death Gaspar is assimilated by the sun and comes to represent an immortal cycle of regeneration. As he turns to stone, a regression takes place from the Maya/Quiché Fourth Age, in which people were made of corn, to the Third Age, when they were made of wood.[3] Nevertheless, García does not adequately explain the end of the novel. Asturias criticism in general has not accounted for the last chapter of the novel, "Correo Coyote," the longest and most discursive of all the chapters. The climactic event of this chapter is the metamorphosis of Nicho Aquino, and the key to an understanding of this crucial event and the ending of the novel is the interpretation of the meaning of metamorphosis to animal form in *Hombres de maíz*.

Metamorphosis as Integration

Four techniques used by Asturias particularly manifest mutability in *Hombres de maíz*: (1) animistic simile and metaphor; (2) imagery of mirroring and shadowing; (3) dream; and (4) "perspectivism," the manipulation of names. Not surprisingly in a novel whose title indicates that its people are made of a vegetable product, rhetorical figures repeatedly suggest the relatedness and consubstantiality of entities of one realm of being with those of another, for example, animal with vegetable, telluric force with animal, solid with liquid, tangible with ethereal, human with a range of nonhuman substances (food, very often). Whether this constant interrelatedness is commented on by a character or established by the omniscient narration, it is calculated to communicate the Indian view of the world as pervasively fluid.

Simile occurs to signal perceived or apparent similarity, and its function is largely pictorial or conceptual.

Alrededor de los fogarones, la noche se veía como un vuelo tupido de pajarillos de pecho negro y alas azules. . . .

(Around the fires the night was like a dense flight of small birds with black breasts and blue wings. . . .)[4]

La guerrilla es igual al fuego de la roza. Se le ataja por un lado y asoma por otro. Se le ataja por ese otro lado y asoma por otro. Guerrear con guerrillas es como jugar con fuego y si yo le pude al Gaspar Ilóm fue porque desde muy niño aprendí a saltar fuegarones, vísperas de Concepción y para San Juan. (*Hombres*, 69)

(Guerrilla warfare is like the flames in the clearing fires, you cut it off on one side and it turns up somewhere else. Fighting guerrillas is like playing with fire, and if I was able to defeat Gaspar Ilóm it's because when I was a small boy I learned to jump over firecrackers come the Immaculate Conception and the Day of Saint John.) (*Men*, 75)

Pleito de arañas parecían las manos del Subteniente bajo el juego de luces y de sombras. (*Hombres*, 75)

(The hands of the second lieutenant looked like squabbling spiders beneath the play of lights and shadows.) (*Men*, 82)

Las gentes son como tamales envueltos en ropa. Se les sale lo colorado. (*Hombres*, 46)

(People are like tamales wrapped in clothes. The red drips out of them.) (*Men*, 47–48)

But Asturias plays on us a trick of major proportions in his use of metaphor, for when the blending of thing and other which is metaphor overtakes the analogy explicit in simile, the thing in Asturias' work actually becomes the other. Let us take one example in which simile slides into metaphor.

Sólo veía las llamas que se escabullían igual que orejas de conejos amarillos, por pares, por cientos, por canastadas de conejos amarillos, huyendo del incendio. . . . Las orejas de los conejos amarillos pasaban sin apagarse por los esteros arenosos de aguas profundas, huyendo del incendio que extendía su piel de ojo pavoroso. . . . (*Hombres*, 44)

(All he saw were the flames scuttling about like the ears of yellow rabbits, in twos, in hundreds, basketfuls of yellow rabbits fleeing from the fire. . . . The ears of the yellow rabbits passed through sandy pools of deep water, unextinguished, fleeing from the fire which stretched out the skin of its dreadful eye. . . .) (*Men*, 45)

The skill of the extended metaphor should not delude us into assigning it a purely pictorial function; the flames really are the yellow rabbits, the yellow rabbits of Gaspar Ilóm's original dream, the allies of the firefly sorcerers and the symbols of golden fertility, of corn. The simile at the beginning of the passage connotes the impression on Tomás Machojón as he views the fire. The transformation of simile to metaphor signals to the reader the double essence of the phenomenon flames/rabbits. Dozens of metaphors function in the novel in the same way as does this one, and one more example should suffice to underline the kind of interpretation they require.

Goyo Yic no alcanzó a llegar a las gradas del corredor, se dejó caer y resbalóse como un cuerpo sin vida por el chaflán de tierra que del camino subía a las gradas. Un muñeco de milpas con ojos de vidrio, estáticos, abiertos, limpios, brillantes. (*Hombres*, 111)

(Goyo Yic didn't make it to the verandah, he fell and slid like a lifeless body down the earth slope which led up from the road to the steps. A maizefield doll with glass eyes, open, clear, shining.) (*Men*, 125–26)[5]

The people of the Third Age, according to the *Popol Vuh*, closely resembled dolls, their faces without expression and their limbs without strength.[6] In this metaphor we are not being told that Goyo Yic resembled a doll, but rather that in essence he was a doll. This difference between correspondence and actual consubstantiality has metaphysical significance in Maya/Quiché thought, as illustrated by an episode in the *Popol Vuh* which inspired a play by Asturias included in *Leyendas de Guatemala*. In the *Popol Vuh*, at the close of the Third Age, Vucub Caquix ("Seven Macaws") decides to proclaim himself the sun, the light, and the moon;[7] but the narrative belies his claims and his vainglory, and he is killed by Hunahpú and Xbalanqué, who are declared to be true gods. In Asturias' drama *Cuculcán, Serpiente-Envuelta en plumas,* Cuculcán (who is for the Mayas the equivalent of the god Gucumatz of the Quiché pantheon and Quetzalcóatl of the Nahuas) is repeatedly tempted by Guacamayo ("macaw") to say that he is the sun. However, Cuculcán will only say that he is like the sun, knowing that to say that he is the sun would be sacrilege. Very much the same principle operates in the use of simile and metaphor in *Hombres de maíz*. If the thing is like the other, a similarity is perceived, and since the Indians are allowed by the gods only partial understanding of earthly reality, that perception may suggest a deeper relationship or simply a superficial analogy. However, the metaphor denotes essential consubstantiality, belonging to transcendental reality.

Imagery of mirroring and shadowing is much less pervasive in *Hombres de maíz* than in *Mulata de tal*, a later novel sometimes considered a sequel to *Hombres*. Nevertheless, mirroring imagery in both novels has the effect of reflecting a deeper, often paradoxical or opposite, appearance to that of the entity that is being mirrored (an effect on the order of that depicted in Picasso's painting *Girl Before a Mirror,* 1932).[8] For example, *aguardiente* is characterized as "líquido que desde siempre ha sido helado y poco móvil, como si guardara en su espejo de claridad la más negra traíción al hombre" (*Hombres,* 44) ("that brew which has always been frozen and still, as if in its clear mirror it held the blackest treachery known to man"; *Men,* 45). But the mirror can refract as well as reflect, and Asturias also nurtures the metaphorical possibilities of refraction,[9] principally during Nicho Aquino's culminating vision of the underworld.

—Las sustancias . . . —se dijo el señor Nicho, al ver pasar aquellas sustancias ígneas, volcánicas en presente vegetal, por el mundo pretérito de los minerales rutilantes, fúlgidos, repartidos en realidad y en reflejo por todas partes, arriba y abajo, por todas partes. (*Hombres,* 249)

("The substances," whispered Señor Nicho, as those igneous volcanic substances flowed by in their vegetable present through that preterite world of twinkling, resplendent minerals, scattered in reality and in reflection, everywhere, high and low, everywhere.) (*Men,* 292)

Shadows somehow seem physically to penetrate the surface, to act as the roots of being and also to suggest the alter essence.

Vas a ver que cuando el Gaspar nadaba, primero era nube, después era pájaro, después sombra de su sombra en el agua. (*Hombres,* 61)

(I tell you, when Gaspar swam, first he was a cloud, then he was a stone, and then the shadow of his shadow in the water.) (*Men,* 65)

Las piedras anaranjadas reflejaban caballos y jinetes, sólo que sus sombras regadas como tinta de tinteros negros, no parecían quedar en la superficie, sino penetrar la piedra. (*Hombres*, 82)

(The orange-colored stones reflected riders and horses, only the shadows spilled like ink from black inkwells seemed not to stay on the surface, but to penetrate the stone.) (*Men*, 90)

Goyo Yic becomes aware of his own metamorphosis by seeing his shadow. Hilario Sacayón, who now guards the treasured secret of Nicho Aquino's transformation, thinks of the nagual as "una especie de coyote suave, de coyote flúido, de coyote oscuridad en cuya sombra se perdían, en cuatro patas, los dos pies del correo" (*Hombres*, 243) ("a kind of soft coyote, a fluid coyote, a coyote of darkness in whose shadow were lost, on four paws, the two feet of the postman"; *Men*, 285).

Neither mirroring nor shadowing concerns the alteration of entities; rather, these two types of imagery, both of which suggest an extension of being, relate to the mode of mutability as "shifting semblance." They are linked, as well, to dream, which has overriding importance in Asturias' work. Dream permits penetration to another level of reality, not only the reality of the unconscious, as André Breton would have it, but the supernatural reality to which all of earthly nature is bound.[10] Asturias believes this aspect of his work to be an imitation of Indian narrative. "The Indian narrative unfolds on two levels: the dream level and the level of reality. Indian texts portray the everyday reality of the senses, but at the same time they convey an oneiric, fabulous, imaginary reality which is seen in as much detail as the other one."[11] This second reality takes the form of revelation in *Hombres de maíz*. Gaspar Ilóm's dream opens the novel, and in it he is accused of allowing the *maiceros* to rob the sleep from the eyes of the land, as though the earth must also have the chance to dream in order to remain sacred.

—El Gaspar Ilóm deja que a la tierra de Ilóm le roben el sueño de los ojos.
—El Gaspar Ilóm deja que a la tierra de Ilóm le boten los párpados con hacha. . . .
—El Gaspar Ilóm deja que a la tierra de Ilóm le chamusquen la ramazón de las pestañas con las quemas que ponen la luna color de hormiga vieja. . . . (*Hombres*, 9)

("Gaspar Ilóm is letting them steal the sleep from the eyes of the land of Ilóm."
"Gaspar Ilóm is letting them hack away the eyelids of the land of Ilóm with axes. . . ."
"Gaspar Ilóm is letting them scorch the leafy eyelashes of the land of Ilóm with fires that turn the moon the angry brown of an old ant. . . .") (*Men*, 1)

On the eve of the catastrophe that is about to befall the people of Ilóm, la Piojosa Grande dreams that two roots, white with the movement of reflec-

Metamorphosis as Integration

tions in the beating water, have penetrated from the green earth to the black earth, from the solar surface to a dark world. There a man attends a banquet. The two white roots tint the amber liquid that the man holds in his hands. But he does not see the reflection of the white roots; he drinks the liquid and falls writhing to the ground, "las uñas casi negras en los dedos amarillos de luna" (*Hombres*, 24) ("his nails almost black against his fingers yellow in the moonlight"; *Men*, 20).[12] The dream has foretold to the woman not only the poisoning of Gaspar Ilóm at the banquet but also the triumph of the moon. Moon (a female principle), shadow, and dream come together again at the critical point when Goyo Yic becomes the *tacuatzina* (*female opossum*).

> De noche al regresar a la posada en sus recorridos de pueblos y ferias, paraba en cada pueblo donde había feria, contemplaba a la luz de la luna su sombra: el cuerpo larguirucho como ejote y la tilichera por delante a la altura de la boca del estómago, y era ver la sombra de una tacuatzina. De hombre al hacerse animal a la luz de la luna pasaba a tacuatzina, a hembra de tacuatzín, con una bolsa por delante, para cargar sus crías.
>
> Se dejó bañar, en una de esas noches de luna en que todo se ve como de día, por la leche de palo que baja de las heridas de la luna macheteada en la corteza, luz de copal que los brujos cuecen en recipientes de sueño y olvido. El copal blanco, misterioso hermano blanco del hule que es el hermano negro, la sombra que salta. Y él hombre/tacuatzín saltaba, blanco de luna, y saltaba su sombra hule negro. (*Hombres*, 115)
>
> (Returning at night to his lodging, during his wanderings through towns and fairs, stopping in every town where there was a fair, he gazed at his shadow by the light of the moon: a long stringy body, like a beanpod, and a tray in front level with the top of his stomach, it was like seeing the shadow of a she-opossum. The moonlight turned him from a man into an animal, an opossum, a female opossum, with a pouch in front of him to carry the babies in.
>
> He let himself be bathed, one of those moonlight nights when everything looks just as it does by day, in the tree milk that flows down from the machete cuts in the bark of the moon, that light of copal the wizards cook in receptacles of dream and oblivion. White copal, which is the mysterious white brother to rubber, the black brother, the darkness that jumps. And the man-possum jumped, white with moon, and his black rubber shadow jumped.) (*Men*, 130–31)

Here metamorphosis occurs as metaphor and as dream arising from both despair and desire. The dream reveals Goyo Yic's essential nature as the one who bears both his children and his vision within, and it also establishes his mythological status as one of the animal gods of the Third Age.

In his own quest for his lost mate, Nicho Aquino cannot fall asleep, and neither, of course, can Benito Ramos, whose pact with the devil precludes the most elementary contact with the sacred. Nicho must renounce his inauthentic way of life definitively before he will be permitted to know the transcendent reality of dream. In his climactic dream-vision of the other world, water (in which flows the collective consciousness, as García has shown[13])—the element in which Gaspar Ilóm became the shadow of his shadow and which reflects and refracts aspects of being—produces the dream of truth.

> La Casa Pintada daba a la orilla de un lago subterráneo. En el agua oscura pequeñas islas de millones de algas verdes, manchas que se iban juntando y separando bajo el pulso ténue de la corriente. Allí, por mucho que el señor Nicho tocara el agua, la realidad era más sueño que el sueño. Por una graciosa abertura, medias naranjas de bóvedas cubiertas de estalactitas y estalagmitas, se reflejaban en el lago. El líquido de un profundo azul de pluma brillante, mostraba en su interior, como en un estuche de joyas las zoguillas del deslumbramiento, los fantásticos calchinitles atesorados por la más india de las indias, la Tierra. Fúlgidas granazones de mazorcas de maíz incandescente. (*Hombres*, 248)

> (The Painted House looked out over the edge of an underground lake. In the dark water floated small islands formed by millions of green algae, masses moving together and parting on the gentle swell of the current. Down there, however much Señor Nicho might touch the water, the reality was more of a dream than dreams themselves. Through a delicately carved opening, arches covered with stalactites and stalagmites were reflected in the lake like oranges cut in half. Down inside the liquid, the deep blue of a gleaming feather, all the glittering necklaces and fantastic gems collected by the most Indian of Indian women, the earth, were on show, as if in a jewelry case. Grains of incandescent maize shed from the most resplendent of cobs.) (*Men*, 291)

And further: "Los que la beben, hombres y mujeres, sueñan con verdes que no vieron, viajes que no hicieron, paraísos que tuvieron y perdieron" (*Hombres*, 249) ("Those who drink it [the rainwater], men and women, dream of greens they have never seen, journeys they have never made, paradises they have had and lost"; *Men*, 292). And surely the most fundamental truth of the world of the people of Ilóm is their crushing loss. Truth, by its nature, is not mutable; mutability in this narrative world consists in the perception that earthly reality is devoid of transubstantiation, that is, that earthly objective reality is not in contact or communication with the other world. The illusion is that reality is made up of entities floating meaninglessly and interchangeably in a vacuum. Mirroring and shadowing imagery and the visions of dream reveal the rootedness of phenomena, the carnal connection between the entities of this world and the truth of the other world; thus the imagery and dreams act, paradoxically, to deny transcendental mutability.

Leo Spitzer, in an essay on Cervantes' *Quijote*, has shown how the manipulation of names in the novel contributes to a sense of mutability characteristic of the classical Spanish Baroque. Spitzer calls this manipulation "perspectivism."[14] This perspectivism challenges any sense of stasis in the earthly order of things but never defies the established Christian metaphysical order as taught by the Church. Thus, at the terrestrial level, "los sueños sueños son," and all is in flux; but in Heaven fixity, stasis, and eternity reign. In Asturias' novel also, we find play with, and confusion about, names. Aleja Cuevas calls Hilario "Canelo" and O'Neill called him "Jobo," both names associating him with a stick.[15] At this point Hilario is, indeed, one of the men of wood. The name of the Irish sewing machine salesman is never fixed. In the interpolated story of the Spanish priest Don Casualidón (*casual* meaning "chance"), the priest gives up a comfortable pastorate for one in a very poor Indian village because according to rumor the Indians pan for gold only to give it away, since for them it is without value. Punished by cruel hardship for his greed, Don Casualidón has given up the priesthood out of remorse. Now he chafes whenever they call him "Sicambro."[16] The real name of Juliantico, the pilot of the boat that goes daily to the island fortress, is Juliancito Coy (*Qoy* meaning "monkey").[17] At the beginning of chapter 6, on discovering his wife missing, Nicho Aquino "la llamará, no como la llamaba cuando eran novios, Chagüita, o como la llamaba después que se casaron, Isabra, sino como se dice a toda mujer que huye, 'Tecuna' " (*Hombres,* 143) ("will call her, not Chagüita, as he called her before they were married, nor Isabra, as he called her after, but what every woman who runs off is called, 'tecuna' "; *Men,* 163).

Of course, the most significant character whose name changes is la Piojosa Grande ("the large lousy one")/María Tecún (the name of an actual mist-covered ridge in central Guatemala)/María la Lluvia ("the rain").[18] The first of her names establishes her identification with the goddess Xmucané (grandmother of the corn, also the lousy one), the second links her to the earth, and the third to an element. Like other techniques conveying mutability, the significance of names has been signaled by Asturias and is seen also in the *Popol Vuh*. During the dice game in chapter 6 of *Hombres* we are told that the men never pronounce the name of the woman they truly care for, since to pronounce the name is to possess her magically.[19] In the *Popol Vuh* Hunahpú and Xbalanqué (his twin) must scheme to learn the names of the lords of Xibalbá (the Underworld) because only thus can the two defeat them. Raphael Girard explains the native idea that "the variants of the name of a deity express distinct functions that it has or performs."[20] For Asturias, then, the name has a magical function; it gives a clue to the essential nature of the being, and the voicing of it confers power. Since the characters in *Hombres de maíz* function on several levels—as themselves, as mythological symbols and metaphorically as elements, as animals, as food—and since some of them can manifest themselves in more than one form, it is appropriate that names should also vary. Nevertheless, as we have seen, mutability is only apparent. The transubstantial essence of each being is stable and immutable; as in the *Quijote*, the metaphysical order prevails and imposes coherence on being.

Turning now from the mutability of the world of *Hombres de maíz* to the individual metamorphoses that occur in that world, we will look first at the meaning of nagualism before proceeding to an examination of the three human/animal pairs—the healer/deer, Goyo Yic/opossum, and Nicho Aquino/coyote—and their experiences. The metamorphoses from human to animal form in *Hombres de maíz* are based on the ancient Mesoamerican belief in nagualism. Some controversy among anthropologists has arisen over what the natives mean by this term. Julian Pitt-Rivers claims that the word is of Nahuatl origin, from the root meaning "to disguise," whereas Benson Saler quotes G. Foster to the effect that *nagual* (of Aztec origin) means "el brujo que se transforma" (the witch who transforms himself).[21] Daniel Brinton, in a monograph written in 1894, assigned to nagualists both indecent and conspiratorial practices (he thought they were a widespread clandestine society), but later anthropologists have found his speculations exceedingly fanciful.[22] Nevertheless, scholars have repeatedly associated nagualism with malevolent magic. It is clear that the use of the term by the natives varies from place to place, and evil practices seem to be assigned to nagualism more frequently in studies of Mexico than in those of the Quiché areas of Guatemala.[23] Saler's research in a Quiché village, Santiago del Palmar in Quetzaltenango, reveals five meanings of *nagual*: (1) an affinity between a particular person and a particular animal; (2) a sign of the zodiac; (3) a sign belonging to the person from his/her date of birth according to the Maya/Quiché calendar; (4) a totem (protector of the community); and (5) a medium that is a spiritual essence.[24] He differentiates between the *nagual*, which is benign, and the *brujo* ("witch") and the *hechicero* ("necromancer"), who use their powers to work evil. Asturias clearly has in mind this benign kind of nagual, defined in the following way by an interpreter of the *Popol Vuh*, Raphael Girard: "An alter ego of a person, of vegetable, animal, human or godlike nature. An inner relationship, fully defined, exists between the person and his or her nahual(s) from birth to death: e.g. a nahual of Hunahpú is the fish. . . ."[25]

Asturias prepares us for the culminating episode of Nicho Aquino's metamorphosis and mystical vision by means of the death of the Venado de las Siete-rozas and his nagual and by the metamorphosis of Goyo Yic. Like Mackandal in *El reino de este mundo*, the Venado is leader, teacher, precursor, and magician. And also like Mackandal, the Venado undergoes martyrdom and resurrection for the benefit of his people. The Venado is the last character to appear in the novel who understands and can interpret the significance of the death of Gaspar Ilóm, and he is the one who will initiate Nicho Aquino into the mysteries of the other world. In the chapter that bears the Venado's name, the many characters who speak—the Tecún brothers, the women of their family, and their neighbors—are fiercely engaged in the struggle against the *maiceros*. By chapter 5, when we meet the next character to be transformed, Goyo Yic, the conflict over the growing of corn has receded, the people have lost their sense of collectivity (each being dedicated to his or her own personal pursuits), and spiritual deterioration has reached an advanced stage. The characters who will undergo transformation henceforth belong to an inferior level in terms of their vision, their spiritual power, and their ability to act. Thus, the death of the Venado, and the events that follow it by one day, recounted in the next chapter, signal the end of an era, the utter defeat of the people of Ilóm and the end of the Fourth Age.

The chapter entitled "María Tecún" departs from the first four chapters not only by virtue of the enormous social changes that it evidences but also in its concentration on the obsessive and agonized inner state of its protagonist, Goyo Yic. Though the Venado is only known objectively, Goyo Yic's inner states are the preponderant subject of this chapter. Goyo Yic's relationship to the opossum is usually similative; he is like the opossum in myriad ways. Only the passage quoted on page 39 of this chapter suggests an actual metamorphosis, and it can be interpreted as simile, as is seen in the English translation. As we have noted, Goyo Yic's body, with the peddler's tray in front of him, casts an opossum shadow. Symbolically he resembles the opossum, which is a marsupial, because he carries the memory of his children, like a burden, within himself. The most significant of his senses, of course, is his vision. As a blind man, he was able to see within; he could see the "flor de amate," an invisible flower, likened by the surgeon to his beloved. The acquisition of his sight propels him into a series of activities, each of which degrades him further as a human being. As a blind man he earned his living partly by gardening and partly by begging alms, the latter being one of the inevitable results of the *ladino* capitalist economy. Once he is sighted, Goyo becomes a capitalist himself, peddling trinkets at fairs. It is at this time that the association with the opossum becomes especially intense. In addition to the actual change that takes place in the moonlight (or does it?), Yic keeps an opossum as a pet until it runs away on the night that he sleeps with a prostitute. Both the lustful union with the woman and the selling of goods for profit specifically violate the moral code of his ancestors. In the next episode he becomes drunk, a further transgression,[26] and it is while he is unconscious of what he is doing that he makes the fateful contract with Domingo Revolorio that results in their imprisonment.

Goyo Yic is the first of the Indian characters from Pisigüilito in the novel to move and to wander. According to Raphael Girard, the Third Age historically was characterized by an abundance of food, burgeoning populations, and consequent widespread migrations; yet the people of this age "still lacked the mental and religious character typical of Maya culture."[27] Asturias exactly captures the character of this age in the chapter "María Tecún," with its evocations of crowds of people in constant movement from one place to another, buying and selling merchandise, services, and their own bodies, and worshipping false gods (several scenes take place in churches, and Goyo Yic prays to the Opossum God). In the *Popol Vuh* the people of the Third Age were destroyed for their wickedness and for their failure to worship the true gods. Thus, in practical terms Goyo Yic's sight enables him to begin his migrations, thereby precipitating his moral failures and cutting himself off from what remain of his cultural roots. Gaspar Ilóm and the pre-*ladino* culture are never mentioned in "María Tecún." Symbolically, the operation to save Goyo Yic's sight, paid for in money—and this point is returned to several times—cannot provide him with moral, religious, and cultural vision because he belongs to a lost age, an epoch in which fertility is a curse and even the family has lost the stuff that binds it.

During his life with his family, in spite of his handicaps, Goyo Yic had led a joyful and purposeful life, and he had provided a modest subsistence for his family. The loss of María Tecún and his children is equivalent to the loss of his soul, and that human soul is replaced by an opossum soul. After his operation, Goyo Yic is impelled "blindly" to wherever he might discover María Tecún. His actions are instinctual and habitual, devoid of caring, of purpose, of meaning. Significantly, he makes the contract with Mingo unconsciously, while drunk, and cannot recall it at all. Eventually even desire and despair desert him.[28] Having lost will, feeling, and human soul, Goyo Yic descends into an existence characterized as "peor lo peor de lo peor" (*Hombres*, 140). Now as a prisoner he is deprived even of freedom of movement and the ability to understand what he has done.

Goyo Yic's similative metamorphosis thus verbally reshapes his body to appear opossum-like. It sharpens his senses only to deaden his spiritual perceptions. And it makes him a prisoner of debilitating forces, first figuratively and then literally. His relation to time also becomes deformed. After his surgery, on the first occasion that he leaves the house to look at the world, he stands on a bridge and gazes at flowing water.

Metamorphosis as Integration

No se veía que el agua se fuera y se iba, sólo comparable con el tiempo que pasa sin que se sienta, como siempre tenemos tiempo, no sentimos que nos está faltando siempre. . . . (*Hombres*, 110)

(You couldn't see the water going, but it went, comparable only with time, which passes without us noticing: as we always have time, we don't realize we are always short of it . . . .) (*Men*, 124)

Thus time flows irretrievably yet meaninglessly. Precious and valuable when lived for the sake of family and community, time loses its very substance for the empty human, and being itself becomes vacant.

In contrast to the objective description of the Venado's doubling and to the suggestion of Goyo Yic's metamorphosis, the transformation of Nicho Aquino is elaborated poetically in all of its existential modalities. The changes of the body, rendered subjectively, provoke the alterations of perception, of the modes of behavior, and of existence in time which are a central subject of investigation here. Section 18, in chapter 6, begins as follows:

En lugar de cabello, pelo de música de flauta de caña. Un pelo de hilos finos que su mano de hoja con dedos peinaba, suavemente, porque al hundir mucho sus uñas, cambiaba el sonido, se le resbalaba como un torrente. Asistía a grandes derramientos de piedra con un sentimiento de ferocidad en la carne de zapote sin madurar y el vello helado, zacate repartido sobre sus todos miembros. La afirmación de una cárcel de fibras musculares tensas, rejuvenecidas, bañadas por lava con rabia de sangre y teniendo de la sangre sólo el rojo puro. . . . (*Hombres*, 243)

(Instead of hair, fur like the music from a cane flute, a coat of fine threads which his hand, a leaf with fingers, combed softly, because when he sank his nails in deep the sound would change and come splashing over him like a torrent. He witnessed great spillings of rock with a feeling of ferocity in his flesh of unripened sapodilla, the icy down wrapped about his limbs like grass. A prison of tight muscular fibers, rejuvenated, washed by lava with a raging of blood. . . .) (*Men*, 285)

Here Asturias depicts synaesthetically the very sensations of metamorphosis from human to animal form. The transformation takes place at the María Tecún ridge, shrouded always in a heavy mist. It is here that la Piojosa Grande turned to stone, and as we remember, she is the embodiment of rain. Again water fulfills its function in accomplishing purgation and renewal. Nicho senses his long teeth, his paws, his tail. He now talks inside himself, with a kind of sucking; otherwise he is mute. He is both astonished and frightened by what has happened to him. As we have seen, one's *nagual* belongs to that person for life, and others had noted the mailman's similarity to the coyote in his swiftness. Here, however, Nicho abandons human form altogether and feels the otherness of the coyote as his own self.

Like Gregor Samsa, Nicho needs time to adjust, time to adapt to new modes of perception and of movement. The scent of his woman fills his nostrils, since this is the magic place where the husbands of "tecunas" feel most powerfully the presence of their lost mates. Typically for the coyote, his body itches, and he strains to scratch. He notices the altered shape of his eyes.

Extraño ser así como era: animal, puro animal. El ojo de pupila redonda, quizás demasiado redonda, angustiosamente redonda. La visión redonda. Inexplicable. Y por eso siempre andaba dando curvas. Al correr no lo hacía recto, sino en pequeños círculos. (*Hombres*, 244)

(Strange to be like him, an animal, purely animal. The round pupil of his eye, too round perhaps, painfully round. Round vision. Inexplicable. And for that reason he always moved in circles. He didn't go straight as he ran, but in little circles.) (*Men*, 286)

The coyote's fierce appetite wells up in him. He does not recognize the two mailbags that are still strapped around him, and he perceives them as two monstrous animals laying hold of him. He struggles, laughing, to set himself free of them. Clearly, the metamorphosis, which occupies three vivid paragraphs, has degraded Nicho Aquino. For the moment he is a beast, having lost his powers of speech and memory (except for the olfactory reminder of his wife) and those of reflection and judgment. It is extreme disorientation, far removed from the willed transformations of Mackandal or Ti Noel. He has not known his *nagual* as had the Venado. Again like Gregor Samsa, Nicho Aquino experiences a forced and inexplicable transformation, but in contrast to Gregor's metamorphosis, Nicho's is a step taken unwittingly toward regeneration.

As an animal, Nicho becomes attuned to the elemental perceptions of his senses. As we have seen, he scratches the itching; he also bites at the mailbags and takes uncertain steps, losing his balance and banging his head and body. He tries desperately to call to the old man, his companion (the Venado), but he is unable to do so. "Nada pudo" (*Hombres*, 244) ("He could do nothing"; *Men*, 287). Thus the transformation severely reduces both sophistication of motive and power to act and in this light also appears as existential debasement.

In terms of time, however, the metamorphosis functions as the beginning of a healing process. The recurrence to immediacy, which is a manifestation common to literary metamorphoses to animal form, serves in this case almost to blot out the past, which is unbearably painful, and the future, which dominates the being of husbands of "tecunas." Upon awakening, the mailman finds himself a human again. But the metamorphosis has left one indelible effect, and that is that time no longer matters for him: "el tiempo que para el señor Nicho ya no ha de contar más" (*Hombres*, 245) ("the time which for Señor Nicho would count no more"; *Men*, 287). Time, which had been measured by the footfalls of his duty and by the hills that served as sundials, will be obliterated now by the renunciation of inauthentic obligation to a society no longer his own and by the journey through the other world where the sun does not shine.

Generalizations about animal symbolism in *Hombres de maíz* and in the *Popol Vuh* must be weighed with extreme care. In the *Popol Vuh* animals in general are punished for not being able to speak and thereby to worship the gods.[29] Furthermore, some of the men of the Third Age are turned into monkeys as punishment, as are Hunbatz and Hunchouén, the vainglorious and envious half-brothers of Hunahpú and Xbalanqué. On the other hand, one of the reasons for which the men of the Third Age are punished in the first place is their cruelty to animals.[30] Thus, animals belong to an inferior order, yet respect for them and caring treatment of them are required by the Maya/Quiché ethical code. The coyote itself plays two significant roles in Maya/Quiché thought. The coyote is one of the four animals that bring the good news about the new food, corn, and it is exactly at this point in the sacred narrative that the men of corn are formed. In effect, according to Girard, the Quiché believe that they learned to eat wild corn from observing coyotes do so.[31] The Sun-Coyote belonged to the primeval religious stratum of northern peoples of the hunter-gatherer cycle. However, in the Maya/Quiché legends the Sun-Sparrow Hawk (Wak-Hunahpú) kills the Coyote (Hunahpú-Utiu) at the beginning of the Fourth Creation, "that is, the animal that symbolized the prehistoric cycle [the coyote] is annihilated by the one representing the Maya-Quiché culture."[32] Thus, both the coyote as bearer of good news and the coyote as god are placed at precisely the point at which the most important transition of culture occurs for the Quiché. The coyote's appearance as culture-bearer and the animal's death coincide exactly with the metamorphosis of a people.

Before going on to a consideration of the summation of the values involved in the mutability of this narrative world and in the metamorphic crisis, we need to take a step back in order to explicate the adventures of the third of the major characters in the last two chapters, Hilario Sacayón. Hilario occupies space equal to that of Goyo Yic and Nicho Aquino and must be granted an importance almost equal to theirs. The question of what he is doing here and what relation he bears to the other two characters must be addressed in order to interpret the novel as a whole. We remember that Hilario is the character who retells the legend of Miguelita, although he feels ambivalent about his story, since he recounts it while inebriated and denies its veracity to himself while sober. We first meet him in the tavern of Aleja Cuevas, and on his journey in search of the mailman he stops at Doña Moncha's inn, sees the coyote at the María Tecún ridge, stops for coffee at a stand in the city, goes to the post office, has his hair cut at a barbershop, meets Benito Ramos in a bar, goes with Ramos to another inn, returns the next morning to the same coffee stand, attends a party at the *rancho* of Candelaria Reinosa, and plays cards at the *rancho* of Don Casualidón. Each stop is characterized by three motifs. First, the places are all dominated by a woman or the image of a woman. Second, in each place he realizes the inauthenticity of one aspect of his life and the life of his society. And third, in each place an incident or legend associated with the ancient cultural roots of his people is awakened in him. In the paragraph that concludes Hilario's participation in the action of the novel, we are told that his character is permanently altered. Possessor of a hidden truth, he becomes sober and circumspect, and he nurtures that profound truth in silence. Nevertheless, we understand that he has become the conscious bearer of knowledge that belongs collectively to his people. Hope that the descendants of the people of Ilóm will come to cultural purity again lives through him. He is the poet (as one character calls him) who may find his tongue and become the "Gran Lengua" if his race can find its way out of the darkness of the Lunar Age.

Clearly, the fates of the other two protagonists of the latter two-thirds of the novel, Goyo Yic and Nicho Aquino, are involved in the destiny of the people of Ilóm as a whole. Several critics have developed theories concerning these two based on myths from classical Greek mythology.[33] Though one hesitates to dismiss summarily such treatments, it is necessary to remember that the preponderance of internal evidence through chapter 5 links the meaning of *Hombres de maíz* very closely to the *Popol Vuh*, and therefore interpretations of the ending that ignore the *Popol Vuh* or depart significantly from it become suspect. In the *Popol Vuh* the people of the Fourth Age worship three gods—Tohil, Hacavitz, and Avilix—and are protected and supported by them. Is there indication of the emergence of these gods in *Hombres*? Goyo Yic is reunited happily with María Tecún and his children at the end of the novel. Significantly, they return to Pisigüilito to farm and to watch their children grow and propagate. Ants, to which they are related metaphorically, are the friends and helpers of Hunahpú and Xbalanqué,[34] indeed ants actually save the lives of the divine twins.[35] Avilix, the third deity of the Cultural Age trinity, is described by Asturias in his translation of the *Popol Vuh* as cultivator and sower of seed and by Robert M. Carmack as having female characteristics and being associated with the moon.[36] We have seen that Goyo Yic embodies all of these attributes. In addition, he bears initials similar to those of Gaspar Ilóm himself and is married to another incarnation of Gaspar Ilóm's own wife, suggesting an undeniable parallel between the Goyo of the end of the novel and the great culture hero. Goyito Yic has been arrested for rebellion against the *ladino* authorities, and thus in him resides the hope that Gaspar Ilóm's uprising will be renewed.

Nicho Aquino undergoes a second metamorphosis after his journey through the other world. He has now made the conscious choice to renounce his inauthentic behavior. (He, after all, was the carrier of paper—always associated with evil in the novel—and of money to the center of *ladino* domination, the capital.) He has also undergone a series of trials and has been initiated into the metaphysical mysteries that rule the being of the people of Ilóm. Now he is split, having become both a coyote roaming the María Tecún ridge and a man. René Prieto interprets his name as "Ak Kin" ("he of the sun") and believes he has become a priest.[37] Asturias renders "Ak" as "lengua" ("tongue") and "Kin" as "sun" or "day."[38] It is surely no accident that on returning to his earthly existence, Aquino goes east to the coast, for it is here that the Quiché people originated and it is here, of course, that the sun originates each day as well. On the coast he achieves a position of dominance, becoming the owner of a hotel, a proprietor (upon the death of the former female proprietor). Hacavitz, the second god of the Fourth Age trinity, is the god of the East and of the sun,[39] and thus Nicho Aquino may be seen as the symbol of Hacavitz.

And what of Tohil, the first god of the Fourth Age pantheon and the prime mover? He is strongly associated with the Venado—the avenger of the massacre of the warriors of Ilóm and the one who accomplishes Nicho Aquino's redemption—because Tohil has promised to manifest himself in the form of a deer. But Tohil, the god of thunder, also appears in the tremendous storm that directly precedes the reunion of Goyo Yic and María Tecún, brought about by Nicho Aquino, who ferries her to the fortress. Thus, Asturias suggests a possible regeneration of the people of Ilóm, an issuing in of the Fourth (or Fifth) Age, resulting from the spiritual apotheoses of Goyo Yic and Nicho Aquino and the emergence of the Fourth Age trinity. Asturias perhaps chose to provide a hopeful rather than a happy ending to his saga of a people because of the still ugly realities of the life of the Indians of contemporary Guatemala.

Metamorphosis to animal form is of two kinds in *Hombres de maíz,* and these are intimately linked to the quest for the woman. The quest reveals itself as a search for wholeness, for existential integrity, and also for a reintegration into a coherent fabric uniting the metaphysical, the natural, and the human. When Goyo Yic loses María Tecún and his soul, his metamorphosis symbolizes his spiritual debasement, and this is the same kind of transformation that Nicho experiences the first time. Nicho's second metamorphosis, which is at the same time a doubling, results in the same kind of being as that inhabited by the sacred Venado de las Siete-rozas. As we have seen, animals in Maya/Quiché mythology are both inferior beings and gods. By fully accomplishing the split between the nagual and the human self, the character comes to participate in the truths of past, present, and future and to embody the metaphysical, natural, and human realms. This second kind of metamorphosis is complete integration on all levels of reality, and it contributes to the task of collective regeneration.

The protagonist of *Hombres de maíz* is the whole people of Ilóm. It is their destiny that concerns us throughout the work. If the novel seems digressive on first reading, it is because we do not recognize the symbolic structure and because we are not accustomed to a collective protagonist. We expect to see the culture embodied in one primary hero. Asturias envisions the problems of this people as a complexity that requires several solutions: an end to the despoiling of the land, a return to subsistence farming, a mystical and historical vision, a renewal of communal effort, and a revitalized awareness of collective myths. All of this is served in the fates of Hilario, Goyo and María, Goyito, and Nicho Aquino. The fundamental truth of the people of Ilóm, that they are the people of corn and all that that signifies, is unalterable, although terrestrial reality is altogether mutable as long as the Indians are cut off from their spiritual sources. The metamorphosis of Nicho Aquino, the climactic event of the novel, symbolizes the possibility of earthly transformation, the potential of the whole people for transcendence and for participation in all realms of reality.

Unlike Ti Noel, who became at the end of *El reino* a prototype for all people, the collective hero of *Hombres de maíz* represents only itself. The world of *Hombres* is a closed world, longing for a return to its own source and cohesion in order to find itself again. Its own particularity and individual identity are what is precious and threatened. Like Thomas Mann in *Doctor Faustus*, Asturias searches the history, culture, myths, and collective mentality of his countrymen and women in order to discover the country's special needs and the origin of its fall.

4 Metamorphosis as Cosmic Refuge
Macunaíma

In *El reino de este mundo* and *Hombres de maíz*, the novel as genre engages myth as paradigm and myth-making as historical process. Reverence for myth enters Carpentier's novella as motive for political change and founds Asturias' novel as precious primordial element vital to the survival of culture. Mário de Andrade's novel *Macunaíma*, on the other hand, although it too grows out of mythical and legendary material, belongs to a different narrative tradition subsumed by the novel, that of satire. Less interested in the social and historical conditions in which Brazilian Indians live than in their legends, music, and dance, Andrade recasts selected folkloric material—especially legends of the Taulipang and Arekuná peoples of Northwest Brazil and Venezuela, collected by Theodor Koch-Grünberg in *Vom Roroima zum Orinoco*[1]—in such a way as to create a pan-Brazilian hero/anti-hero and to signal, to lament, and to deride certain aspects of Brazilian national life and character. Haroldo de Campos, one of several outstanding interpreters of *Macunaíma*, has analyzed the novel in the light of Vladimir Propp's *Morphology of the Folktale*.[2] According to Campos, at the same time that Propp was studying the Russian folktale in order to construct his morphology of the basic elements common to all folktales, Andrade was studying the Brazilian folktale in order to create his meta-tale.

De fato, operando com sinal inverso em relação a Propp, Mário tratou, por assim dizer, de recombinar as "variantes" de uma fábula virtual, de base, numa polimorfa metafábula. A "polimorfia", salientada por Propp no estudo do seu material, convertia-se, para Mário de Andrade, não numa dificuldade a superar, para fins de clarificação metodológica, mas, precisamente, no horizonte fascinante aberto aos seus desígnios de invenção textual, de "texto-síntese".

(In fact, operating inversely with relation to Propp, Mário tried, one could say, to recombine the basic "variants" of a potential folktale into a polymorphous metafable. The "polymorphousness," emphasized by Propp in the study of his material, became for Mário de Andrade, not a difficulty to overcome, for the purposes of methodological clarification, but rather, precisely, a fascinating horizon open to his designs for textual invention, for a "text-synthesis.")[3]

In his study Campos convincingly demonstrates that Andrade, having grasped the same fundamental structures that Propp systematically delineates, incorporates those structures into *Macunaíma* in such a way as to form an intricately and authentically ordered myth/legend/satire/novel. As Emir Rodríguez Monegal has pointed out, the use of myth in *Macunaíma* links it to *Hombres de maíz*: "Los dos libros han propuesto algo similar: el rescate de una mitología y una cosmovisión que aunque aparentemente destruída por la cultura occidental sigue viva en las entrelíneas del texto de la realidad latinoamericana" (The two books have proposed something similar: the rescue of a mythology and a cosmovision which, although apparently destroyed by occidental culture, remain living between the lines of the text of Latin American reality).[4]

Mário de Andrade has referred to *Macunaíma* both as satire and as rhapsody. Although ambivalent about the symbolic nature of his hero, the author admits that by subtitling the work "O herói sem nenhum caráter," he identifies the mode of the novel as satire.

E resta a circumstância da falta de caráter do herói. Falta de caráter no duplo sentido de indivíduo sem caráter moral e sem caraterístico. Está certo. Sem esse pessimismo eu não seria amigo sincero dos meus patrícios. E a sátira dura do livro. Heroísmo de arroubo é fácil de ter. Porêm o galho mais alto dum pau gigante que eu saiba não é lugar propício prá gente dormir sossegado.

(And there remains the circumstance of the lack of character of the hero. Lack of character in the double sense of individual without moral character and without characteristic. Yes. Without that pessimism I would not be a sincere friend to my compatriots. This is the tough satire of the book. A rapturous heroism is easy to have. But the highest branch of a gigantic tree which I might know of is not a propitious place for people to sleep peacefully.)[5]

But *Macunaíma* is satire in the original sense of the Latin word *satura* ("mixture") as well. The novel is a mélange, a fusion of extremely disparate levels and regions of discourse. In order to create a sense of pan-Brazilianism, Andrade incorporates words from various Brazilian Indian and African languages as well as street language, formal literary language, technological words, magical and mythical words, baby talk, folk songs, comic words, coined words, and obscenities. Both the thrust of the satire and the daring linguistic mix are meant to shock and unsettle, and they belong rightfully to the literary revolution that characterizes Brazilian Modernism. When Andrade uses the words *rapsodismo* and *rapsódicas* in the first preface to *Macunaíma*, he both explains the style and excuses the sexual explicitness (he calls it pornography) of the book as typical of religious books and popular rhapsodism.

Quanto a estilo, empreguei essa fala simples tão sonorizada música mesmo por causa das repetições, que é costume nos livros religiosos e dos cantos estagnados no

Metamorphosis as Cosmic Refuge 53

rapsodismo popular. Foi pra fastarem de minha estrada essas gentes que compram livros pornográficos por causa da pornografia. Ora se é certo que meu livro possui além de sensualidade cheirando alguma pornografia e mesmo coprolalia não haverá quem conteste no valor calmante do brometo dum estilo assim.

(As for the style, I used such simple, sonorous, musical language exactly because of the repetitions, which are the custom in religious books and of the songs stagnated in popular rhapsodism. It was to drive away those people who buy pornographic books for the sake of the pornography. Now if it is true that my book goes beyond sensuality, smelling of some pornography and indeed of obscenity, there will not be any one who can contest the calming value of the bromide of a style such as this.)[6]

Rhapsody thus refers to the oral, popular, folkloric sources to which *Macunaíma* is heir and also draws on the musical connotations of the term as a composition irregular in form, seemingly an improvisation. The first edition of *Macunaíma* (1928) is specifically called "historia" ("tale"), but Andrade changed the designation of the second edition (1937) to "rapsódia." In the third (1944) and subsequent editions the title page has simply read *Macunaíma: O herói sem nenhum caráter*.[7]

In order for us to clarify the ways in which modern satire interweaves with indigenous legend in the rhapsody, it will be helpful to examine a key episode in some detail. Chapter 8, "Vei a Sol," is based on a Taulipang legend collected by Koch-Grünberg.[8] According to the legend, in ancient times there existed a very high tree. Walo'ma, the frog, climbed to the highest point in the tree. A man named Akalapijeíma waited every afternoon at the foot of the tree to catch the frog. Walo'ma said that if Akal were to catch him, he would throw him into the sea. The man caught him, and Walo'ma dragged the man through the water to an island, leaving him there. The *urubus* (Brazilian black vultures) defecated on him until he was smeared and stinking. Being very cold, Akal appealed to the morning star to take him to the sky, but she refused because he had always offered mandioca cakes to the sun but never to her. Then he asked her for fire and again was told to ask the sun. He asked the moon either to return him to his own land or to give him fire, but the moon also directed him to the sun. Then Wei the sun came and took Akal into his canoe, ordering his daughters to wash him and to cut his hair. Wei wanted him for a son-in-law. Akal asked Wei to warm him, and Wei crowned himself with a headdress of parrot feathers, carrying Akal higher and higher in the sky. When Akal became too hot, Wei gave him clothes to cool him. Wei warned Akal not to involve himself with other women so that he could marry one of the daughters of the sun, but when Akal returned to earth, he fell in love with the daughters of the *urubus*. Wei became very angry and told Akal that if he had followed Wei's advice, he would have stayed young and handsome. Now he would grow old and die. "[Akal] foi nosso ancestral, o pai de todos os índios. Por isso ainda hoje vivemos assim. Ficamos jovens e bonitos por tempo muito curto, tornando-nos então feios e velhos" ([Akal] was our ancestor, the father of all of the Indians. That is why we live as we do. We stay young and handsome for a very short time, then become ugly and old).[9]

Andrade closely follows the basic outline of this myth of the loss of immortality, giving the name "Volomã" to the tree itself and making it the antagonist. That is, the vegetation itself is fruitful, yet unyielding. Nevertheless, Macunaíma, cast here in the role of Adam assaulting a reluctant Tree of Life, utters the incantation, "Boiôiô, boiôiô! quizama quizu" (*Macunaíma*, 65), which, according to M. Cavalcanti Proença, is the Indian name of the tree,[10] and he thereby forces the angry tree to give up its fruits. The tree, in turn, hurls Macunaíma beyond the bay of Guanabara to a deserted island formerly inhabited by Alamoa, an evil nymph who came to Brazil with the Dutch. Macunaíma falls asleep in midair. Like Akal, he is lambasted in his sleep by the *urubus* and wakes up cold. Thus, for violating the first interdiction Macunaíma is punished by being hurled into cold isolation and attacked by the excrement of birds of death. Furthermore, he is asleep and it is night. Alamoa, being associated both with the Dutch colonialists and with greed, is the first sign of foreign intervention in Brazil in the chapter, and Macunaíma has no hesitation in seeking her treasure. Instead of the treasure, however, he finds only a species of ants. He asks the morning star to take him to heaven, but the star answers, "Vá tomar banho" (Go take a bath), thus inventing a common expression used by Brazilians to address certain European immigrants (also an expression of disbelief or discontentment). The moon also refuses to help and directs him to the sun. In the novel Vei is feminine, and she is good to Macunaíma because she remembers that he always offered mandioca cakes to her. The sun and her daughters clean and comfort him, and desiring him for a son-in-law, the sun offers him "Oropa, França e Bahia" as a dowry if he will renounce other women. Soon after their arrival in Rio de Janeiro, however, Macunaíma, left alone, takes up with a Portuguese woman. In defiance he declares, "Pois que fogo devore tudo! . . . Não sou frouxo agora pra mulher me fazer mal" (To hell with everything! . . . I'm not so flabby that a woman can hurt me) (*Macunaíma*, 68). Then he utters what will be his definitive and repeated denunciation of the evils by which his country is beset. "POUCA SAÚDE E MUITO SAÚVA, OS MALES DO BRASIL SÃO" (Too little vigor and too many ants are the troubles of Brazil) (*Macunaíma*, 68).[11] Just as in the legend, when Vei discovers his betrayal, she tells him he has lost his chance for

Metamorphosis as Cosmic Refuge 55

immortality. He protests that he was lonely and "if he had only known." Vei then gives him the Vató stone, but he trades it for a picture in the paper.

Thus, in the novel the sun grants several benefits to Macunaíma and holds out the promise of more. She cleans and purifies him, symbolically restoring him to life. She offers him love, leisure, contentment, and, implicitly, immortality. She also brings him to the city. There he finds his own companionship and has no need for her stone/fire. As Telê Lopez explains:

A pedra vató, em contato com a sociedade de máquina, perde o valor que tinha para a obtenção do fogo entre os primitivos das lendas: Macunaíma se desfaz dela. E elemento acessório e de existência circumstancial e ilustrativa, ao contrário da pedra muiraquitã, essencial na ação do romance.

(The *vató* stone, in contact with the society of the machine, loses the value it had for the acquisition of fire among the primitives of the legends: Macunaíma gets rid of it. It is a superfluous element, of circumstantial and illustrative significance, as opposed to the *muiraquitã*, which is essential to the action of the novel.)[12]

Macunaíma trades tropical fulfillment for intercourse with a Portuguese woman, a contravention so powerful that he pays for it not just by aging and by being beset by a monster but also by being mutilated at the end of the novel in Vei's final ambush.

Macunaíma's lack of character thus originates in the legends themselves, but it is carefully and consistently adapted to the modern character of his country. He exploits nature by force, consorts with colonial interests, goes back on his word, trades the durable for the ephemeral, and sets individual desire as the prime motive for action. Andrade, then, not only preserves the beauty and the richness of the Indian legends but also stretches them in such a way as to explore their potential for expressing contemporary psychological, ethical, and political concerns. As in the works of Carpentier and Asturias, a return to indigenous culture in *Macunaíma* opens a new route toward an understanding of modern heterogeneous and colonized culture.

Mutability especially expresses itself in *Macunaíma* by (1) the collapsing of space and time, (2) the operations of manipulative and mythical magic, and (3) the recurrent motif of a lost Golden Age, which, as in Ovid's *Metamorphoses*, gives the sense of entities having formerly been other and of culture in transition.

We do not know the date of Macunaíma's birth. It is lost in the darkness of the primeval forest. Chronology in the first four chapters and in the last three is measured by Macunaíma's personal growth—which is affected several times by magic and metamorphosis so as to obfuscate any perception of natural human development—and by his decline at the end of the story. His constant recourse to popular wisdom and his teachings of Indian belief, indeed his use of magic itself, show Macunaíma to be an original source of ageless knowledge, and we are told at the end that he is the descendant of the *jaboti*, the first of all the races.[13] Furthermore, except for the deepening sadness over the loss of Ci and the changes resulting from the alteration in skin color, Macunaíma's personality experiences very little growth from the beginning of the book to the end. On the other hand, the chapters during which Macunaíma inhabits the city (chapters 5–14) belong to a specific historical period (the mid-1920s), clearly designated by the naming of machines and gadgets of the era. Thus, city time and jungle time are carefully distinguished, the former being characterized as a microcosmic moment in history, the latter as a macrocosmic, mythical process slowly moving toward eventual decline.

In both spheres realistic perceptions of time are constantly subverted, coinciding with subversions of spatial relationships. Here M. M. Bakhtin's concept of chronotope is a useful tool for analysis.

> We will give the name chronotope (literally, "time space") to the intrinsic connectedness of temporal and spatial relationships that are artistically expressed in literature. . . . In the literary artistic chronotope, spatial and temporal indicators are fused into one carefully thought-out, concrete whole. Time, as it were, thickens, takes on flesh, becomes artistically visible; likewise, space becomes charged and responsive to the movements of time, plot and history. This intersection of axes and fusion of indicators characterizes the artistic chronotope.[14]

Macunaíma may be seen to have the following five major chronotopes: (1) the virgin forest, whose passage of time has been described above; (2) the city street, which has also been characterized; (3) the pension that Macunaíma occupies in São Paulo and other enclosed dwellings (the sun's boat, the *malocas* in which Macunaíma lived with his family and with Ci), whose time is defined by Macunaíma's labored interaction with others, his expressions of melancholy, his illnesses; (4) the points of encounter with the Piaimã and other characters who at the same time belong to legend and to the realm of social satire—the cannibals, i.e., the currupira, Ceiuci, Oibê (The most important of these is the house of the giant in São Paulo, to which Macunaíma returns five times. The places are usually situated with a geographical exactness, for example, "Venceslau Pietro Pietra morava num tejupar maravilhoso rodeado de mato no fim da rua Maranhão olhando pra noruega do Pacaembu" [Venceslau Pietro Pietra lived in a marvelous hut surrounded

Metamorphosis as Cosmic Refuge 57

by woods at the end of Maranhão street facing the valley of Pacaembu] [*Macunaíma*, 39]. Time in these latter episodes is filled in by frantic action, intrigue and deception, rapid metamorphoses, and the chase); and (5) the sky, about which more will be said later in this chapter.

The fourth chronotope most especially illustrates the collapsing of space and time in *Macunaíma*, and we find one of the important manifestations of this chronotope in chapter 11, "A Velha Ceiuci." Toward the end of this chapter Macunaíma goes fishing in the Tietê and is caught by Ceiuci, the Piaimã's wife. Rescued by her younger daughter, who then becomes a comet, Macunaíma sets out to flee the old woman, who is the *caapora* (an evil forest goblin).

This chase returns us to an issue raised in the Introduction, that is, the opposition set forth by Carpentier between authentic American magic and the so-called contrived magic of Surrealism. Macunaíma starts out from the giant's house in São Paulo on horseback.

Caminhou caminhou caminhou e já perto de Manaus ia correndo quando o cavalo deu uma topada que arrancou chão. No fundo do buraco Macunaíma enxergou uma coisa relumeando. Cavou depressa e descobriu o resto do deus Marte, escultura grega achada naquelas paragens inda na Monarquia e primeiro-de-abril passado no Araripe de Alencar pelo jornal chamado Comércio do Amazonas. Estava comtemplando aquele torso macanudo quando escutou "Baúa! Baúa!". Era a velha Ceiuci chegando. Macunaíma esporeou o cardão-pedrês e depois de perto de Mendoza na Argentina quasi dar um esbarrão num galé que também vinha fugindo da Guiana Francesa, chegou num lugar onde uns padres estavam melando.

(He galloped and galloped and galloped and near Manaus he was moving rapidly when the horse stumbled and pulled up some ground. At the bottom of the hole Macunaíma caught sight of something shining. He quickly dug it up and discovered the remains of the god Mars, a Greek sculpture found in those parts back in the time of the Monarchy and last April Fool's Day in Araripe of Alencar by the journal named Comércio do Amazonas. He was contemplating that wonderful torso when he heard, "Baúa! Baúa!" It was the old woman Ceiuci coming up behind him. Macunaíma spurred on the spotted horse and after almost running into a galley which was fleeing from French Guiana near Mendoza, Argentina, he came to a place where some priests were making honey.) (*Macunaíma*, 98)

During the chase, Macunaíma crisscrosses Brazil several times, touching most, perhaps all, of the states of the country at least once, entering Argentina and Peru and nearing the borders of Bolivia, Uruguay, and Paraguay. He finds the statue (an actual find had been reported in the newspapers and then dismissed as an April Fool's joke), meets a galley (presumably of slaves), is hidden by Argentinian priests, deciphers or does not decipher

Indian rock inscriptions in various parts of the country, is hidden by the *surucucu* (the largest of Brazil's poisonous snakes)—whom he rewards with a ring turned into four hundred contos worth of carts of millet, some manure, and a secondhand Ford—meets a woman hiding from the Dutch (since the time of the wars with the Dutch, 1640–1654), and finally is brought home by the *tuiuiu* (wood ibis) who metamorphoses into an airplane. We do not know how long the journey lasts, but he meets the *surucucu* on the fourth day.

The flight of Macunaíma recalls the flight of Lautréamont's Maldoror as the latter outsmarts and outlasts the police by being today in Madrid, tomorrow in St. Petersburg, yesterday in Peking.[15] As we have seen, Carpentier attacked Lautréamont and the Surrealists for the absence of popular faith, myth, and history in their versions of the fantastic. The flight of Macunaíma, and indeed the entire tale of his adventures, provide, perhaps, a necessary intermediary between the revolutionary myth of Mackandal, grounded in recent history, and the purely imaginary Maldoror (who nevertheless rebels against authentic currents of European intellectual history). Macunaíma is a genuine folk hero, borrowed by Andrade from tribal legend and adapted to a new series of modern adventures perfectly in keeping with the hero's more ancient deeds and his traditional personality. Andrade simply contemporizes the legend and thereby gives it renewed meaning.

The chase chronotope telescopes extensive geographical space into a conceivable, graspable whole, a unity that can be reduced to the sum of its parts. Overwhelmed, as one must be, by Brazil's magnitude and diversity, Andrade nevertheless conceptualizes Brazil and its culture as a totality, one set within the larger totality of Latin America.[16] The statue of Mars in the passage quoted above refers to a magazine article about the discovery of fragments of a marble statue near Manaus, perhaps a representation of Mars, and the inscriptions to contemporary theories that such inscriptions were left in Brazil by the Phoenicians.[17] The aid tendered by animals situates Macunaíma in the legendary plane, whereas the references to priests, galleys, the Monarchy, and the Dutch place him in history. Thus time in the chase chronotope, as well as space, is disjoined and telescoped, and in addition, at least three types of discourse used to record and interpret human activities—journalism, legend, and history—are evoked and fused.

The old woman Ceiuci is the wife of Venceslau Pietro Pietra, thus a capitalist. She is also a cannibal, a theme to which we will return in the discussion of the Golden Age. Telê Lopez, in her excellent study of Andrade's intellectual life, outlines the theme of the old woman as one of major interest to Andrade in his collections of popular stories, ballads, and songs.[18] These materials treat the old woman as faded beauty and lost fertility. For Andrade

Metamorphosis as Cosmic Refuge 59

the old woman is a remnant of ancient matriarchal systems, now brought low, feared and ridiculed. This chase sequence thus embodies two manifestations of mutability that operate in *Macunaíma* at once. The old woman's threat is cannibalization, a particularly fearful form of mutability and one that functions both at the primitive, carnal level and at the modern, economic level. But furthermore, this chronotope creates both a geography corresponding in its detail to actual places, displaced and rearranged into an imaginative cohesion, and a history fused to legend and reordered into a digestible, comic, otherworldly chronology.[19]

The second of the major principles of mutability operating in *Macunaíma* is magic, and although many entities and characters employ magic in the novel, the principal magic users are Macunaíma and his brother Maanape, the sorcerer. Macunaíma's magical manipulations are often connected to the breaking of taboos, and the view of taboos in the novel is almost certainly derived from Freud's *Totem and Taboo*, which Andrade probably read in 1925.[20] Macunaíma turns himself into a prince, for example, in order to have sex with his sister-in-law (incest); he moves the family hut to higher ground in order to be alone with his mother (and it was really with her, instead of Sofará, that he wanted to frolic in the jungle). Several times he turns Jiguê into a telephone, which violates a taboo against consorting with machines, a transgression against the ethical code of the novel. In the Macumba episode he uses magic against the Piaimã, who can be interpreted as a father figure to the fatherless Macunaíma. In the legends collected by Koch-Grünberg, the giant is the father of magic and the master magician who teaches young apprentices his arts (see legend 21, for example). He is a cannibal and the personification of darkness, and his conflicts with Makunaíma represent solar and lunar eclipses. Thus his large size, his status as constant older antagonist, the fact that Macunaíma sleeps with his daughter, make of the Piaimã a dominant, patriarchal, father image. Macunaíma's use of magic against him and his eventual killing of him thus represent the breaking of another most powerful taboo.

Many of the breakers of taboos in *Macunaíma*—for example, Ci, who as an Amazon is required to remain a virgin; the Piaimã's daughter, who betrays her parents and Macunaíma himself—metamorphose into heavenly bodies at points of crisis. In addition, we learn that Carlos Gomes, who had been a famous composer, is now a little star in the sky. This latter remark serves to link the breaking of taboos with artistic creativity. The legendary Makunaíma was the great creator and transformer.

Makunaíma é, como todos os heróis tribais, o grande transformador. Transforma pessoas e animais, algumas vêzes por castigo, na maior parte, porém, pelo prazer da maldade, em pedras. . . . Também é criador. Ele fêz, como já foi dito, todos os animais de caça, bem como os peixes. Após o incêndio universal, que liquida todos os homens, cria novos homens. Nesta tarefa, inicialmente, apresenta falta de habilidade. Modela-os em cêra, de forma que, expostos ao sol, se derretem. Depois os modela em barro para em seguida transformá-los em homens.

(Makunaíma is, like all tribal heroes, the great transformer. He transforms people and animals, sometimes as punishment, mostly, however, for the pleasure of the mischief, into stones. . . . He is also creator. He made, as we have already said, all the animals of prey, as well as the fish. After the universal fire, which destroys all men, he creates new men. In this task, initially, he shows a lack of skill. He models them in wax, so that, exposed to the sun, they melt. Later he models them in mud in order subsequently to transform them into men.)[21]

Thus, it is in the fundamental nature of Andrade's hero to work magic, to transform, to create. However, it is the satiric aspect of this modern Macunaíma that begins to predominate in many of the episodes in which he uses his magic, for we begin to have a foreboding that the light-hearted contraventions of modern "tribal" and "natural" laws may have catastrophic consequences. Although Macunaíma is the great hero, he is human enough to suffer. Since Macunaíma's implementation of magic is connected to the breaking of prohibitions, its results for him are either minimal (the black magic of the Macumba wounds but does not kill the Piaimã) or it brings short-term pleasure and long-term punishment (he enjoys sex with Sofará but is triply punished by Jiguê by being beaten, deprived of food, and separated from Sofará).

Maanape, on the other hand, is the tribal healer. His beneficent magic resurrects Macunaíma three times after, in each case, Maanape had warned him against doing the things that would cause him to be killed. Maanape cures Macunaíma's wounds and restores him from illness. Maanape is, as well, the mediator between Macunaíma and Jiguê and is the wise possessor of secret knowledge. Unlike his brothers, he knows no women, enters into no conflict. He is the sage, the healer, the peacemaker. In social terms, magic as practiced by Macunaíma and Maanape has opposite effects. Macunaíma's magic is usually at the service of individualistic goals and it is often mischievous as well. It separates him from the community and makes him an isolated figure. Maanape's magic, however, derives from the ancient practices of his tribe and is a support and a comfort for others. It unites and gives continuity to the community. Magic, then, as mutability principle, has to do with creation and transformation and has far-reaching social and ethical implications as well.

The concept of a golden age and of culture in transition in *Macunaíma* relates both to Oswald de Andrade's "Manifesto antropófago," published in the first number of the *Revista de Antropofagia*, along with an advertisement for the forthcoming *Macunaíma* (May 1928),[22] and to the ideas about cultural epochs expressed by Count Hermann Keyserling in *The World in the Making*. In his prose-poem manifesto Oswald (no relation to Mário) sets up a dialectic between, on the one hand, prehistoric primitivism, which for him was matriarchal and cannibalistic, sensual, leisurely, and ruled by the collective, and, on the other hand, the historical period, which is patriarchal and slave owning, logical, imperialist, and dominated by the father figures: conqueror, priest, and capitalist. The manifesto calls for revolution and return.

Queremos a Revolução Caraíba. Maior que a Revolução Francesa. A unificação de todas as revoltas eficazes na direção do homem. Sem nós a Europa não teria sequer a sua pobre declaração dos direitos do homem.
A idade de ouro anunciada pela América. A idade de ouro. E todas as girls.

(We call for the Carib Revolution. Greater than the French Revolution. The unification of all the successful revolts in favor of man. Without us Europe would not even have had its poor declaration of the rights of man.
The golden age announced by America. The golden age. And all the "girls.")[23]

According to Telê Lopez, Mário de Andrade did not consider himself part of the *Antropofagia* group, but he could associate himself with their celebration of the primitive and of Brazilian-ness.[24] And we shall see in the conclusion to this chapter that Mário had in mind a similar kind of matriarchal/patriarchal dialectic in the composition of *Macunaíma*.

Count Keyserling's book describes the contemporary period as the age of the chauffeur, an age of mechanistic, as opposed to spiritual, consciousness. Nevertheless, he believes the latter kind of age may and will come. The age of the chauffeur believes in progress, "the range of whose vision is so much narrower and shallower [than the Romantic Age of Hegel]. Briefly explained, it stands for nothing more than this: that the material, moral and mental circumstances of our life shall completely satisfy life's meaning," a crude and barbarous belief to Keyserling's way of thinking.[25] At another point he calls the chauffeur the "technicalized savage."

In *Macunaíma* we find constant reference to past ages. In chapter 10, for example, Macunaíma, outraged by a patriotic speech on the nature of the Southern Cross, takes over the speaker's platform. He explains that the constellation known as the Southern Cross is really the *Pai do Mutum* (father or original ancestor of the *mutum*, a Brazilian species of pheasant), and he tells the Indian legend of the origin of the constellation. In the course of the speech, he makes reference to two separate past ages, one in which animals were people, "like us," and the age in which the legend itself took place.

According to Koch-Grünberg, the primitive concept of animals does not differentiate man and animal, although the primitive imagination settles on the special characteristics of each animal. He indicates that the "primitive era" was an earlier epoch, the time of Makunaíma and the other legendary beings and occurrences.[26] Our Macunaíma, the hero of Andrade's novel, inhabits three ages (that is, he moves imperceptibly from one to another almost simultaneously): the primary age in which animals are undifferentiated from humans (he, after all, speaks often with animals and communicates their messages to others), the following age in which he recognizes that animals were once people but are now a separate order of beings, and the third age which is contemporary and corresponds to Keyserling's mechanized age.

One of the most consistent motifs of the novel is Macunaíma's interaction with machines. When he first arrives in São Paulo, he perceives machines as an order of beings new to him and as the centers of power. Therefore, he sets out to have sex with them in order to conquer them, as he had done with Ci. In the end he is symbolically conquered by the pernicious charms of mechanization, for as he leaves São Paulo for the last time he takes with him to his native region a Smith & Wesson revolver and a Pathek watch. Of these two he makes his ear-pendants and from his lower lip he suspends the *muiraquitã* (the talisman given to him by Ci).

Thus in *Macunaíma*, time and distance contract into themselves so that Brazilian history and geography may be conceptualized as a unity that transcends the seeming separation of regions, cultures, language groups, and historical periods. Magic pervades action, functioning both as individualistic evil and as collective benefit. And culture is seen in helter-skelter transition from primitive cultural purity to mechanized and colonized corruption. Mutability as structural principle provides the novel with a sense that chaos, diversity, and magnitude can be overcome, at least intellectually; and mutability as satire warns against social tendencies and transformations that are perhaps more problematic for Brazil than the "muito saúva e pouca saúde" of which Macunaíma so often complains.

The individual metamorphoses of Macunaíma and other characters participate in the various modalities of mutability in the narrative world described above and bear their own existential meanings as well. The many metamorphoses of Macunaíma form a pattern that finds parallels in the metamorphoses of other entities and culminates in the most significant and crucial transformation, that is, the last one.

As has already been noted, Makunaíma, the hero of the Taulipang and Arekuná legends, is the great transfomer. In addition, when missionaries translated the Bible into these languages, they named Christ "Makunaíma."[27] Thus, the hero of the novel, in his status as originator, inheritor, and transmitter of legendary culture, is rightfully endowed with powers of metamorphosis. He personally undergoes eleven metamorphoses before the final one, and often they occur in groups of three. (He also experiences death and resurrection three times.) He becomes a prince three times in order to frolic with Sofará; he changes into an insect, a plant, and then a man in order to frolic with Iriquí; he becomes an ant (*caxipara*, male *saúva*) in order to harass Venceslau Pietro Pietra; he turns into a fish three times to try to steal the Englishman's fishhook; and then he becomes the *piranha*, which enables him finally to lay hold of the hook. These minor metamorphoses allow him to satisfy instinctual desires in artful and comic ways, for Macunaíma is never satisfied with the mundane. They are spicy and frivolous. The last metamorphosis, however, is entirely other; it makes Macunaíma's story and life, if not tragic, surely profoundly poignant. In addition, to the extent to which Macunaíma embodies Brazil, his final metamorphosis is a painful and despairing vision of the destiny of that nation.

Although Macunaíma is in some ways a super-human character and although he is objectified and satirized, he may be said to embody a self in two of the ways described in the Introduction. He embodies a distinct spatio-temporal history, which he remembers and carries with him, and he is a unity that comprehends contradictions. Remembering Johnstone's definition of the self as one who can know what he or she is to do and not do it, we note in Macunaíma the propensity for lying, which he cannot explain, and his excuse to Vei: "If I had only known." With regard to the third characteristic of selfhood—the ability to reflect on one's own self and being—Macunaíma, although capable of introspection, refuses to engage in it, both out of pride and because he is a man of action. On the other hand, in his second preface to *Macunaíma*, Andrade asserts that Macunaíma represents the *Sein* ("Being") of Keyserling.

Me repugnaria bem que se enxergasse em Macunaíma a intenção minha dele ser o herói nacional. E o herói desta brincadeira, isso sim, e os valores nacionais que o animam são apenas o jeito dele possuir o "Sein" de Keiserling, a significação imprescindível a meu ver, que desperta empatia. Uma significação não precisa de ser total pra ser profunda. E é por meio de "Sein" (ver o prefácio do tradutor em *Le monde qui naît*) que a arte pode ser aceita dentro da vida. Ele é que fez da arte e da vida um sistema de vasos comunicantes, equilibrando o líquido que agora não turtuveio em chamar de lágrima.

(It would repel me if in Macunaíma were to be seen any intention of mine to make of him a national hero. He is the hero of this plaything [the novel], yes, and the national values that animate him are only his tendency to possess the "Sein" of Keyserling, an indispensable meaning to my way of thinking, which arouses empathy. A meaning does not need to be total in order to be profound. It is by way of "Sein" (see the translator's preface to *Le monde qui naît*) that art can be integrated into life. It is what makes of art and life a system of communicating vessels, balancing the liquid that I now do not hesitate to call tears.)[28]

This *Sein* stands in opposition to "action" in Keyserling's terms because action is associated with a lack of sensibility, consciousness, conscience, and spirituality. In Andrade's novelistic adaptation of Keyserling's ideas, we can see that Macunaíma is emphatically a man of feeling, that he leaves his conscience on an island before entering the city (and when he returns for it, he takes that of a Spanish American instead), and that his spirituality consists in his sense of and respect for ancient tradition and in his intimate relations with the creatures of nature and the cosmos.

In the analysis of changes of body, perception, will, and time, Macunaíma must be considered at three levels of representation: as human, as hero, and as symbol. To take the form of a constellation is to give up motility and all forms of relating physically to the world. He will no longer eat, sleep, be sick, fight, flee, hunt, fish, or frolic. His sole physical manifestation will be purely to shine, to give off light (at night, which is associated with hunger, cold, loneliness and death, as we have seen in the analysis of chapter 8). "Ia ser o brilho bonito mas inútil porém de mais uma constelação" (He was going to be the brilliance, pretty but useless, of one more constellation) (*Macunaíma*, 144). He says he did not come into the world to be a stone. By removing himself from earth, he deliberately cuts himself off from contact with vegetable, animal, and especially human forms. As a collection of points of light with an animal name, he rejects any further involvement in human-ness. In Heideggerian terms, he gives up "care," which is the function of Being-in-the-World. As hero, Macunaíma remains in full view of all, tricking some into thinking he is the Saci because of his one leg.[29] He has recovered his other parts (after being dismembered in the pool by the *piranhas*), and they will be visible along with his ear-pendants, the revolver, and the clock. Symbolically, his corporal transformation suggests inertia and stasis. However, the inertia is not the *lazer* related to artistic creativity. It is sterility, spiritless emanation.

We have seen that Macunaíma's sensory perceptions are acute and highly developed, but they reach satiation and then begin to torture him. At the end of the book he cannot bear the heat of the sun, the cold of the water, his nagging sexual desires. At the next level of perception, his emotional life is in ruins. He is lonely and heartsick, and he can find no more resources within himself to change his condition. Unlike Carpentier's Ti Noel, he has no final flash of insight, no introspective leap. His transformation signals his despair. Yet he displays no sign of guilt or remorse because he does not reflect on his past actions any more than he does on his current condition. His consciousness remains at the affective level, unable to attain the realm of judgment. And it is this lack of judgment, of self-criticism—manifested by his lack of foresight and insight, as well as by his breaking of taboos—that leads to his disastrous final disillusionment. Without judgment, one cannot have "character," for character, in the ethical sense, presupposes the ability to weigh alternative possibilities and to choose according to a system of values. For Andrade, this aspect of Macunaíma's character is indigenous to the Brazilian national character. According to Telê Lopez, Andrade believes, as a result of his studies of popular forms of social criticism, that the Brazilian's ability to analyze and to criticize stops at well-meaning irony and sarcasm.[30]

O reconhecimento do povo brasileiro como primitivo e incaracterístico se deu através do confronto entre observação do cotidiano e situações-amostras que recolheu na literatura popular. Compreende que a impregnação de elementos europeus, de psicologia europeia, oriundos da colonização, ou da imitação, se levados ao exagêro, culminariam com as águas geladas do Uraricoera, deglutindo Macunaíma, o incaracterístico. O exemplo de brasileiro em seus traços mais marcantes: indolência, sensualidade, preferência pelo sonho, observação melancólica da realidade, malícia e agilidade de raciocínio quando em perigo, mentira, pode ser destacado por Mário de Macunaíma e outros personagens indígenas, de Malazarte, do Saci.

(The recognition of the Brazilian people as primitive and without character came from the comparison between his observation of daily life and typical situations that he collected from popular literature. He comprehends that the impregnation of European elements, of European psychology, originating from colonization or imitation, if carried to the extreme, will culminate in the icy waters of the Uraricoera, swallowing up Macunaíma, the characterless. The representation of the Brazilian in his most salient features: indolence, sensuality, preference for sleep, melancholy observation of reality, malice and quick-wittedness when in danger, lying, can be pointed out in the Mário of Macunaíma and other Indian characters, of Malazarte, of the Saci.)[31]

At the human level, we see Macunaíma all too disposed to act out of impulse, instinct, desire. Yet paradoxically, as we have noted, he is meant to personify not action, but being, in Keyserling's sense of the word. Macunaíma is moved to action by discomfort, but his ultimate goal is always inaction, or at least play (especially sexual) or profit. His complaints against ants and ill health are ironic and result from his feeble powers of analysis, for the true impediments to his goal of leisurely contentment are the father figure/cannibal/capitalist Venceslau, and the matriarchal tropical sun Vei, whose friendship he throws away precisely through his lack of character.

Pathetically, the inaction of the useless star will comprehend neither play, nor music, nor sex. It will be being in its purest form, empty presence.

In its temporal dimension, Macunaíma's final metamorphosis represents a contrast both to Ti Noel's final choice and to Nicho Aquino's. Ti Noel elects a human death and assumption into the natural cycle of decay and reification. Nicho Aquino's metamorphosis allows transcendence and eternal participation in the fullness of natural and divine mysteries. On the other hand, Macunaíma, as human, simply stops, and his extinction is the extinction of his people. In his role as tribal hero, as we have seen, he embodies the comprehensive past of his people and is spokesperson as well. In this capacity he survives, for the memory of his existence continues in literature, and his presence will eternally manifest itself in the evening sky. As symbol of Brazil, Macunaíma represents the continuity of ancient Indian traits in the contemporary, multi-racial society. According to this formulation, it is a society that lives for its present, unable to plan systematically for the future, indeed negating the value of such planning. For the Brazilian the present moment achieves richness and meaning in being, not action, in contemplation and feeling, rather than in successive accomplishments. The temporal paradox reveals itself in the nothingness and vacuity of any future unforeseen and unprepared for. Macunaíma's final metamorphosis turns out to symbolize the nihilistic destruction of destiny by a people accused of being without character.

Having established the personal, existential meaning of Macunaíma's metamorphosis, we need now to analyze the transformational crisis in the full context of the values of the narrative world. The two keys to this perspective are the metamorphosis of Macunaíma's brothers and the parable of Taína-Cã, which Macunaíma relates to the parrot directly before his final confrontation with Vei and his metamorphosis. In these episodes we return to the dominant themes of the novel: leisure/work, creativity/sterility, life/death, earth/heaven, indigenous Brazilian culture/colonial culture. These dualities in some ways closely resemble those that come into play in the metamorphosis and death of Ti Noel and the conclusion of *El reino de este mundo*.

Macunaíma leaves the city for the last time with his foreign, manufactured acquisitions (not just the revolver and the clock but two Leghorns, a foreign hybrid, as well), thinking like an engineer: "Pois então Macunaíma adestro na proa tomava nota das pontes que carecia construir ou consertar pra facilitar a vida do povo goiano" (Then Macunaíma, resting in the prow, took note of the bridges which needed to be built or repaired to make life easier for the people of Goiás) (*Macunaíma*, 121). As a city dweller, he has become enormously creative, not the least of his creations being new words,

Metamorphosis as Cosmic Refuge 67

as we shall see. However, on his return to his native region, he falls ill with malaria. Indeed, he no longer lives in harmony with these surroundings. Whereas before he had had enormous energy and extraordinary magical powers for sexual activities, hunting and fishing, now he does not have the strength, the talent, or the will. He foils his brothers' efforts to provide for the group as well and schemes to poison Jiguê. Once Jiguê has become the shadow, he swallows both Maanape and the princess (who is a metamorphosed tree). As the shadow/Jiguê pursues Macunaíma, the latter comes upon an ox (*boi*), which he kicks, causing a stampede of oxen. In the confusion Jiguê attaches him/herself (shadow [sombra] is feminine) to the ox and proceeds to eat all of its food. The ox finally dies, and there is great rejoicing among all the species of vultures and buzzards. They dance and sing around the rotting corpse, and then they feast on it. Jiguê becomes the second head of the Father of the Vultures.[32]

The *boi* is a sacrificial animal in many regions of Brazil, especially in the northeastern states, and Andrade took a particular interest in the sacrificial ceremonies, making an extensive collection of folk songs about the *boi*.[33] In his marginalia to the tenth chapter of Frazer's *The Golden Bough*, "Relics of Tree Worship in Modern Europe" (which Andrade read in French), Andrade signals what he considers to be a parallel between European vegetation/fertility rites and Brazilian rituals among cattle-herding communities. He concludes that since Brazil has its economic focal point in cattle rather than in the earth, the value of the ox is raised to mythical status.[34] "O Boi mal comparando, parece assumir uma posição de Dionisio, símbolo de reflorescimento e do tempo fecundo" (The ox, comparing loosely, seems to assume the position of Dionysus, symbol of reflorescence and fertile season).[35] And again: "O Boi é realmente o rei do criação" (The ox is truly the king of creation).[36] Indeed, he goes even further and declares: "O boi é realmente o principal elemento unificador do Brasil" (The ox is truly the principal unifying element of Brazil).[37] The death of the Boi in Brazilian festivals produces rejoicing, popular singing, and dramatic dances which are at the same time communal and primordial to native tradition. Furthermore, each part of the ox's body is committed to a practical use benefiting the collectivity.[38] In *Macunaíma* Andrade rewrites the ceremonies to make the collectivity a community of vultures. By so doing he represents, as Carpentier was to do later, the natural cycle of animals consuming others, death giving life. As we have seen in the chapter on Vei, the defecation of vultures leads the human being to seek light, warmth, and cleansing, and these comforts, in turn, drive him back to union with the birds of death. And so the cycle perpetuates itself. In effect, then, Jiguê and Maanape are consigned to the cycle of nature and belong eternally to the earth.

In contrast, Macunaíma makes the choice that was available to Ti Noel, which the latter rejected, that is, transformation into an unearthly, eternal form, breaking with the natural cycle. In Macunaíma's parable of Taína-Cã, he spells out some of the implications of that choice. Taína-Cã is the evening star, and Imaerô, the older daughter of a Carajá chief, fell in love with him because of his beauty and brilliance and wanted to marry him. One evening he presented himself to her in human form, and they became engaged. Her younger sister Denaquê was very jealous. The next day, however, Taína-Cã appeared old and wrinkled, and Imaerô refused to marry him. Denaquê, on the other hand, accepted him, and they were married. Taína-Cã, in spite of his aged looks, was very energetic sexually, and he made Denaquê idyllically happy. Every day Taína-Cã would leave their hut and would tell Denaquê not to follow him. He was clearing land and planting, which was something new and unheard of by the Carajá. He would go back and forth from earth to heaven bringing back everything that the Carajá lacked. But Denaquê began to follow him, and she fell in love with other, little, stars. Saddened and embittered by her infidelity, Taína-Cã returned to heaven and stayed there. "Si a Papaceia [Taína-Cã] continuasse trazendo as coisas do outra lado de lá, céu era aqui, nosso todinho. Agora é só do nosso desejo" (If the evening star had continued bringing things from the other side, the sky would be here, all ours. Now it is only our desire) (*Macunaíma*, 142).

According to the myth, the separation of earth and heaven came about through betrayal; paradoxically, Macunaíma partakes of all three participants in this drama. He is Imaerô, who cannot recognize true value, for he was seduced by the glitter of technology. He is Denaquê, the unfaithful, for he has betrayed the values of primitivism, the collectivity, his mother, his brothers, the tropical sun. He is also Taína-Cã, for he has been both provider—intermediary between humans and natural forces—and potent sexual force. His story illustrates also the futility of work, agriculture being the destruction of the hunter-gatherer culture to which Macunaíma truly belongs. Thus, the beginning of agriculture, indeed of progress, results in material and spiritual loss and leads eventually to the advent of the technicalized savage.

As Telê Lopez points out, according to Andrade's understanding of Indian culture, the Indians' indolence is linked to creativity, specifically to verbal creativity.

A violenta atividade verbal da criação literária do povo brasileiro corresponde á sua indolência para com atividades laboriosas e sistemáticas. Para Mário ela seria um reflexo do índio como povo formador, desligado que era de uma economia de consumo. A indolência do índio é ressaltada pelos cronistas da Colônia, pelos viajantes do Império e por Gilberto Freyre, sociólogo seu contemporâneo.

Metamorphosis as Cosmic Refuge

(The violent verbal activity of the literary creation of the Brazilian people corresponds to their indolence with regard to arduous or systematic activities. For Mário it [the indolence] is a reflection of the Indian as a creative people, unconnected as he was to a consumer economy. The indolence of the Indian is emphasized by the chroniclers of the Colony, by the travelers of the Empire, and by Gilberto Freyre, his sociologist contemporary.)[39]

One day, while he is living in São Paulo, a flower vendor gives Macunaíma a flower for his buttonhole, but since Macunaíma does not know the word for button-hole, he falls into confusion and irritation, finally blurting out the word *puíto* (an Indian word for anus). The flower vendor repeats the word, and soon Macunaíma discovers that all of São Paulo is calling buttonholes "puítos." He also studies languages and writes the hilariously inventive letter to the Amazon women. Thus, Macunaíma's *preguiça* (his laziness) is of value; it is something that is especially harmonious with his nature, since he is the great transformer and verbal artist. However, since he misuses his magical powers, as we have seen, his leisure becomes progressively sterile and uncreative as it becomes more and more isolated. In addition, for all of his frolicking, he engenders only one child, who is the fruit of transgression and must die. Andrade was emphatic in his belief that art must be involved in social concerns.

O ideal seria então o artista só publicar aquilo que sua consciência social reputa bom e sua consciência pessoal reputa belo? E um engano, R. F., porque ambas estas duas consciências são contraditórias. Quem tem a segunda é um egoísta, que se indiferentiza no individualismo e não pode obter a primeira. E esta primeira despreza a segunda e a repudia. *A lealdade pra com a consciência social é a única que nobilita o artista, e o justifica satisfatòriamente em sua humanidade. E por ela que o artista faz a arte evoluir, pois êle está consciente que transformando a arte, corresponde a uma precisão pública.*

(The ideal would be, then, for the artist only to publish that which his social conscience reckons good and his personal conscience reckons beautiful? This is a fraud, R. F., because these two consciences are contradictory. Whoever has the second one is an egoist who becomes indifferent in individualism and cannot achieve the first. And this first despises the second and repudiates it. *The loyalty to the social conscience is the only thing that ennobles the artist and satisfactorily justifies him in his humanity. It is because of it that the artist makes art evolve, for he is conscious that by transforming art, he is responding to a public need.*)[40]

Leisure, life, and art come together as a vitally dynamic union in the young Macunaíma. In the progression of Macunaíma's career, Andrade dramatizes the decline of the individualistic artist.

As we have seen, *preguiça* is one of the gifts of the tropical sun. Before his initial encounter with Vei, Macunaíma was her special favorite, and we have seen as well that the legendary Makunaíma was even a sun-figure himself. Haroldo de Campos, because of his concern with Proppian structures in *Macunaíma*, points to Venceslau Pietro Pietra as Macunaíma's principal antagonist.[41] However, the tropical sun, not the *muiraquitã*, is the key to happiness and fulfillment for Macunaíma and the Brazilian, according to Andrade's ethic. The defeat of the father is relatively insignificant as compared to the magnitude of the conflict with the mother. Here, for a second time, we find the theme of metamorphosis closely tied to the conflict between male and female dominance. In *Hombres de maíz*, the metamorphosis of Nicho Aquino signals the decline of the matriarchal age. In *Macunaíma*, the metamorphosis of the hero occurs directly as a result of the matriarchy's reassertion of her power. In *Zona sagrada* we will find yet another, this time pathological, linkage between metamorphosis and matriarchy.

Angel Rama has described Mário de Andrade as the founder of the new Latin American narrative.

El orden narrativo que pone en juego, siendo verosímil, nunca es meramente realista. Se gobierna con leyes que fijan un distanciamiento, se organiza al parecer caprichosamente, pero siguiendo rígidas leyes que animan el juego.

Hay en este manejo de la literatura (que estaba siendo el modo en que Kafka venía tratando los "particulares" narrativos desde *La metamorfosis*) una secreta, no confesa supeditación al subjetivismo. Este ensambla el conjunto y lo unifica por una mirada del autor: ella es candorosa y humorística a la par. La levedad de este material, su apariencia inconsútil, juguetona y hasta ingenua, la limpieza y pulcritud de la composición, la constante humildad del asunto y de su tratamiento, no disimulan la sabiduría de un estilo con el que se pone en movimiento la narrativa nueva del continente.

(The narrative order which he puts into play, being probable, is never merely realistic. It is governed by laws that fix an objectivity, organizes itself as though capriciously, but following rigid laws that put the game into motion.

There is in this handling of literature [which was the way in which Kafka was treating the "peculiar" narratives from *The Metamorphosis* on] a secret, unconfessed subduing of subjectivism. This joins the whole and unifies it through one look by the author: it is candid and humorous at the same time. The lightness of this material, its seamless appearance, playful and ingenuous, the cleanness and beauty of the composition, the constant humility of the subject and its treatment, do not hide the wisdom of the style with which he sets in motion the new narrative of the continent.)[42]

Being satire, *Macunaíma* is both comical and didactic. Throughout this chapter we have been concerned with the ethical code because satire by its very nature demands attention to ethics. Nevertheless, *Macunaíma* serves as an appropriate transition between works in which metamorphosis is involved in myth and magic (*El reino* and *Hombres*) and works in which it is involved in play and the game ("Axolotl" and *Zona sagrada*). *Macunaíma* may be considered a legitimate forerunner of Magic Realism in Latin American literature, and it prefigures the Boom as well.

5 Metamorphosis as Creation Game
"Axolotl"

Para mí escribir forma parte del mundo lúdico.

—Julio Cortázar

Metamorphosis in the two remaining narratives to be considered occurs less as a function of myth than as an element of game. Although a political commitment to non-European subcultures is not a predominant feature of Cortázar's "Axolotl" and Fuentes' *Zona sagrada*, a mark made by the anthropological aspect of the metamorphoses discussed in the previous chapters is discerned. As we shall see, Fuentes is preoccupied with the archetypal, ritual nature of game. In the case of Cortázar, game has to do with transition, with the passage from one sphere of experience to another: from adolescence to adulthood, from sanity to madness, from art to life, from dream to waking, from life to death. Cortázar explores both the symbolic and the experiential resonances of game. According to Johan Huizinga, play or game is characterized by freedom: it is voluntary, set apart from ordinary or "real" life, and distinguishable from "appetitive" behavior. In its higher forms play belongs to the sacred sphere. Game is played out within specific limits of space and time (what Fuentes will call the *zona sagrada*), and it endures as a "new-found creation of the human mind," as tradition. Endowed with an inner structure, game demands "absolute and supreme order"; it tends to be beautiful and captivating; it creates an air of secrecy. The player of the game acts a role. In its rhythm and harmony game is related to the realm of the aesthetic. The game is threatened at any time by the potential reassertion of ordinary life in its sphere.[1] Cortázar's story "Axolotl" belongs to his collection *Final del juego* (End of the Game), in which all of the stories explore psychological and existential modalities of game.[2]

David Lagmanovich has admirably summarized five recurring themes in Cortázar's stories, and these coincide precisely with the conception of mutability described in this book. First, Cortázar's stories reveal a contrast between the world of daily reality and another world which intrudes on the first. This intrusion implies the acceptance of the frailty (*caducidad*) of logic, of the other world as normal. The "order" of the real world is substituted by an inexplicable "other" order. Second, the limits between human and animal are explored. The intuition exists that reality is a continuum that challenges the categories of occidental logic. Third, the idea of the double is actively explored. It not only duplicates but also frustrates and inverts the actions of the *I*. Fourth, the categories of space and time are distorted. Time, instead of being linear, is simultaneous or displaced, so that different planes can touch. Space, instead of being discrete, may become continuous, susceptible of being traversed or nullified by an intuition close to magic. Fifth, the contacts between life and art are made more intense. They are conceived of as two planes that are not necessarily separable or distinguishable.[3]

It is a commonplace of Cortázar criticism that animals are one of the primary vehicles in his fiction for representing another reality, a realm of experience alien to the human.[4] However, Cortázar's principal concern—especially in "Axolotl" but also in others of his animal stories—is with the point which lies exactly in between two realms of experience, the nexus of transition. Cortázar's celebrated preoccupation with adolescence is one example of this concern with the point that lies between. He explores the possibilities of crossing the median point (and many of his adolescents die, of course), the dangers that the crossing engenders, and the areas of overlap between the two or various spheres. It will be helpful to describe briefly this focal point of transition, specifically with reference to animal/human bonding, in two stories from *Bestiario*. In "Carta a una señorita en París," the narrator writes a letter to a woman whose apartment in Buenos Aires he is occupying while she is staying in Paris. This man has the bizarre habit of occasionally vomiting baby rabbits (*conejitos*, pointedly, not grown rabbits). Before moving into the apartment he had vomited about one rabbit a month, a singularly idiosyncratic event routinized. Furthermore, the rabbits created for him a routine of feeding and setting free. He feared that the further regimentation of life in the apartment might cause him to vomit the rabbits more frequently, and indeed it does. Soon he has produced eleven rabbits which he must hide from the housekeeper during the day and care for at night. They are endearing little creatures while young, but soon—"ya feos y naciéndoles el pelo largo, ya adolescentes y llenos de urgencias y caprichos" (now ugly and growing hairy, now adolescents filled with urges and mischief)—become unmanageable. The narrator becomes ever more agitated and distraught, unable to control the vomiting or the rabbits. Eventually they destroy the apartment, and the narrator throws himself out of the window. In the following passage we find at least eight images of transition, of passages in between.

Interrumpí esta carta porque debía asistir a una tarea de comisiones. La continúo aquí en su casa, Andrée, bajo una sorda grisalla de amanecer. Es de veras el día siguiente, Andrée? Un trozo en blanco de la página será para usted el intervalo, apenas el puente que une mi letra de ayer a mi letra de hoy. Decirle que en ese intervalo todo se ha roto, donde mira usted el puente fácil oigo yo quebrarse la cintura furiosa del agua, para mí este lado del papel, este lado de mi carta no continúa la calma con que venía yo escribiéndole cuando la dejé para asistir a una tarea de comisiones. En su cúbica noche sin tristeza duermen once conejitos; acaso ahora mismo, pero no, no ahora—En el ascensor, luego, o al entrar; ya no importa dónde, si el cuándo es ahora, si puede ser en cualquier ahora de los que me quedan.

(I interrupted this letter because I had to attend to some commissioned work. I am continuing it here at your house, Andrée, under a still grisaille of dawn. Is it really the next day, Andrée? A blank space in the page will be for you the interval, scarcely the bridge that links my yesterday's hand to today's. To tell you that in that interval everything has fallen apart, where you see the easy bridge I hear breaking the furious band of water, for me this side of the paper, this side of my letter doesn't continue the calm with which I was writing you when I left to take care of the commissioned work. In their cubicle night sleep eleven little rabbits; perhaps right now, but no, not now—in the elevator, then, or coming in; it doesn't matter any more where, if the when is now, if it can be in any of the nows which remain to me.)[5]

The narrator is a *trans*lator by profession, so that the reference to his work has to do with crossing boundaries. The letter, the dawn, the blank space on the page, the bridge, the elevator, and the "when [which] is now" all focus on the point in between. The rabbits originate as an integral part of the man himself and gradually become a sinister Other. At one point the rabbits are pointedly compared to a poem: ". . . un mes es un conejo, hace de veras a un conejo; pero el minuto inicial, cuando el copo tibio y bullente encubre una presencia inajenable. . . . Como un poema en los primeros minutos, el fruto de una noche de Idumea: tan de uno que uno mismo . . . y después tan no uno, tan aislado y distante en su llano mundo blanco tamaño carta" (. . . a month is a rabbit, it really makes a rabbit; but the initial moment, when the warm and lively little cotton ball conceals an inalienable presence. . . . Like a poem in its first moments, the fruit of a night of Idumea: just as much oneself as one is . . . and later so alien, so apart and distant in its flat white world the size of a letter) (*Bestiario*, 24). The crossing of boundaries is extraordinarily dangerous, for it threatens a fragmentation of the self into irretrievable otherness. Yet the temptation to cross is at times imposed, as in this story, and at times irresistible, as in "Axolotl." The linkage of the animal with the poem forms a fundamental bond between "Carta a una señorita en París" and "Axolotl," as we shall see.

In the story "Bestiario," the point in between is the distance between antagonists, and Cortázar explores how it is established and how maintained. A girl, Isabel, (probably prepubescent) goes to the country to visit relatives. Theirs is a somber household which must always remain aware of where the tiger is (in what room or if in the garden) so as not to confront it. Isabel and her young cousin Nino create an ant farm, placing two separate ant colonies in the same glass container. The ant colonies, although aggressive, keep their distance from each other, just as the members of the family do. Isabel realizes that her young Aunt Rema, whom she both loves and admires, is deeply unhappy because of the unnatural attentions of her harsh and brutal older brother Nene. One night Isabel becomes part of the tension between the siblings (she carries to Nene a glass of lemonade in place of Rema, although Nene has expressly ordered Rema to serve him), and the experience of being the intermediary is so acute as to make her feel suddenly removed from the games and projects of her younger cousin. The next day Isabel lies about the whereabouts of the tiger, and Nene is eaten alive. In this story, again, the child hits a transition point in her development; this is also one of Cortázar's stories in which dream and imagination sometimes provide the terrain for the blending of realms of experience.

El formicario valía más que todo Los Horneros [the country house], y a ella le encantaba pensar que las hormigas iban y venían sin miedo a ningún tigre, a veces le daba por imaginarse un tigrecito chico como una goma de borrar, rondando las galerías del formicario; tal vez por eso los desbandes, las concentraciones. Y le gustaba repetir el mundo grande en el de cristal, ahora que se sentía un poco presa, ahora que estaba prohibido bajar al comedor hasta que Rema les avisara.

(The ant farm was better than all of Los Horneros, and she delighted in thinking that the ants came and went without fear of any tiger; sometimes she would imagine herself a tiger as tiny as an eraser haunting the galleries of the ant farm; perhaps because of this the disbandings and the concentrations [of the ant troops]. And she liked to replicate the big world in the glass one, now that she was feeling a little like a prisoner, now that it was forbidden to go down to the dining room until Rema called.) (*Bestiario*, 149)

Here the macrocosmic tiger, which haunts the lives of the humans and in a sense has them caged, is reduced to the level of the ants, themselves imprisoned by humans, again by the mediation of Isabel, since she is both the dreamer and the tiny tiger. Thus, distances are maintained either willingly or by force because crossing the line that separates individual from other, human from tiger, tiger from ant, ant colony from ant colony, threatens destruction.

Doris Sommer has made reference to the similarity between the predicament of Gregor Samsa in Kafka's *The Metamorphosis* and those of Cortázar's protagonists.[6] Certainly the narrator who vomits rabbits resembles Gregor Samsa in that his extraordinary physical condition is both of unknown origin and absurd, and the presence of the tiger at Los Horneros is likewise inexplicable and disturbing. Furthermore, neither the rabbits nor the tiger yield to allegorical interpretation. Jaime Alazraki writes of Cortázar's animal images:

The reader senses . . . that Cortázar's axolotl is a metaphor (a metaphor and not a symbol) that conveys meanings unconveyable through logical conceptualizations, a metaphor that strives to express messages inexpressible through the realist code. The metaphor (rabbits, tiger, noises, axolotl, beggar) provides Cortázar with a structure capable of producing new referents, even if their references are yet to be established or, to use I. A. Richard's terminology, the *vehicles* with which these metaphors confront us point to unformulated *tenors*. We know we are dealing with vehicles of metaphors because they suggest meanings that exceed their literal value, but it is the reader's task to perceive and define those meanings, to determine the tenor to which the vehicle points.[7]

"Axolotl," like the other stories in *Final del juego*, embodies the configurations of game and of animal as metaphorical vehicle and, especially, the problems of the focal point at which transition takes place. All of these configurations have at their core fundamental existential and aesthetic concerns, which may be explicated in terms of the alterations of body, perception, will, and time and by the focus on the transformational crisis. "Axolotl" is the story of a man who goes one day to the aquarium at the Jardin des Plantes in Paris and becomes fascinated with the axolotls. In the opening paragraph he tells us that now he is an axolotl. He remembers having returned to see the axolotls daily until the transformation took place. The narration arises mostly from the point of view of the man, but occasionally it shifts, even in midsentence to the consciousness of the animal: "Vi un cuerpecito rosado y como translúcido (pensé en las estatuillas chinas de cristal lechoso), semejante a un pequeño lagarto de quince centímetros, terminado en una cola de pez de una delicadeza extraordinaria, la parte más sensible de nuestro cuerpo" (I saw a small and seemingly translucent body [I thought of the little China statuettes of milky crystal], similar to a small lizard of fifteen centimeters, ending in a fish tail of extraordinary delicacy, the most sensitive part of our body).[8] At the end of the story the point of view is that of the axolotl, who hopes that the man, who now comes less often to the aquarium, will write a story about the axolotls. Here a metamorphosis undoubtedly takes place because the man's consciousness and self occupy, or are, the axolotl, at least for a time. However, a split eventually occurs: the man is able to walk away, but the axolotl retains as part of its self the man's "obsession," that is, a vivid moment of his consciousness.

The minute descriptions of the modalities of the axolotl/self are sometimes objective from the man's point of view, sometimes subjective from his perspective, and also sometimes subjective from the stance of the axolotl. Before entering into his own extraordinary perceptions of the axolotls, the narrator relates what he has learned about these animals from the dictionary. They are larval forms, provided with gills, of a species of batracian of the

Metamorphosis as Creation Game

genus *ambystoma*. Although he does not further explain, it is essential to the story to understand that the axolotl, though closely related to the salamander, is a very unusual species because it never undergoes metamorphosis. That is, unlike the salamander, which as an adult is amphibious, the axolotl remains at the larval stage and cannot survive out of water.[9] Nevertheless, the axolotl, although an eternal child, does indeed reproduce. As he goes more frequently to the aquarium, the man notes the axolotls' golden eyes, the small pink and translucent bodies. Along the back runs a transparent wing (*aleta*) which fuses with the tail. But what especially calls his attention is the fineness of the feet which end in tiny fingers and nails "minuciosamente humanas." The face is inexpressive, having only eyes: "dos orificios como cabezas de alfiler, enteramente de un oro transparente, carentes de toda vida pero mirando, dejándose penetrar por mi mirada que parecía pasar a través del punto áureo y perderse en un diáfano misterio interior" (two orifices like the heads of pins, entirely of transparent gold, lifeless but looking, allowing themselves to be penetrated by my look which appeared to pass through the golden point and lose itself in a diaphanous interior mystery) ("Axolotl," 123–24). A very thin black halo surrounds the eye. The mouth is obscured by the triangular shape of the face, yet its considerable size can be guessed from the profile. Where there should be ears, three red branches, as of coral, grow; these are the gills.

From beginning to end the description stresses the inanimateness of the creature. The narrator compares the animal to the China statuettes, to a little statue corroded by time and to coral. The head is "la piedra rosa de la cabeza" (the pink stone of the head) and later "la piedra sin vida" (the lifeless stone). Since the gills move, they are "lo único vivo en él" (the only living thing in it). A little later the man states emphatically, "No eran *animales*" (They were not *animals*). This creature, which becomes more and more bizarre and sinister as the story progresses, itself embodies the point in between, arrested transition. It is the adult child, the inanimate animal, the "still life" (*naturaleza muerta*).[10] Yet part of the fascination that the protagonist feels for the axolotls has to do with a sense of kinship:

No eran seres humanos, pero en ningún animal había encontrado una relación tan profunda conmigo. Los axolotl eran como testigos de algo, y a veces como horribles jueces.

(They were not human beings, but in no animal had I found such a profound relationship with myself. The axolotls were like witnesses of something, and at times like horrible judges.) ("Axolotl," 127)

The act of looking takes on momentous significance because for the narrator's part, it is his vision that deepens his penetration into the otherness of the axolotl, and for the animal's part, the gaze allows it literally to devour the man's being.

Los ojos de los axolotl me decían de la presencia de una vida diferente, de otra manera de mirar. Pegando mi cara al vidrio (a veces el guardián tosía, inquieto) buscaba ver mejor los diminutos puntos áureos, esa entrada al mundo infinitamente lento y remoto de las criaturas rosadas. Era inútil golpear con el dedo en el cristal, delante de sus caras; jamás se advertía la menor reacción. Los ojos de oro seguían ardiendo con su dulce, terrible luz; seguían mirándome desde una profundidad insondable que me daba vértigo.

(The axolotls' eyes spoke to me of the presence of a different life, of another way of looking. Pressing my face to the glass [sometimes the guard coughed, uneasy] I tried to see better the diminutive golden points, that entrance into the infinitely slow and remote world of the pink creatures. It was useless to tap the glass with my finger in front of their faces; they never displayed the least reaction. The golden eyes kept on burning with their sweet, terrible light; they kept on looking at me from an unfathomable depth which gave me vertigo.) ("Axolotl," 125)

"Usted se los come con los ojos", me decía riendo el guardián, que debía suponerme un poco desequilibrado. No se daba cuenta de que eran ellos los que me devoraban lentamente por los ojos, en un canibalismo de oro.

("You eat them with your eyes," the guard, who must have thought me a little unbalanced, would say to me laughing. He didn't realize that they were the ones who were devouring me slowly through the eyes, in a cannibalism of gold.) ("Axolotl," 127)

It is the power of the gaze that seems to effect the actual transformation. The objects that lie physically between the man and the animals are the glass of the cage and the water.

Mi cara estaba pegada al vidrio del acuario, mis ojos trataban una vez más de penetrar el misterio de esos ojos de oro sin iris y sin pupila. Veía de muy cerca la cara de un axolotl detenido junto al vidrio. Sin transición, sin sorpresa, vi mi cara contra el vidrio, en vez del axolotl vi mi cara contra el vidrio, la vi fuera del acuario, la vi del otro lado del vidrio. Entonces mi cara se apartó y yo comprendí.

(My face was pressed to the glass of the aquarium, my eyes were trying once more to penetrate the mystery of the golden eyes without iris or pupil. I saw from very close the face of an axolotl stopped against the glass. Without transition or surprise, I saw my face against the glass, instead of the axolotl I saw my face against the glass, I saw it outside of the aquarium, I saw it on the other side of the glass. Then my face moved away and I understood.) ("Axolotl," 128)

Metamorphosis as Creation Game

Unlike the other images of nexus points—letters or bridges, for example—the glass and the water are transparent, that is they permit immediate perceptual penetration. They have no blocking power; they eliminate the defenses of space and time. Since transformation or transition, passage to the other reality, takes place by means of visual perception, that faculty takes precedence over other faculties in the relation between self and other and also gives a clue as to the direction the interpretation of the tenor must take.

For this is a story of conflict, of aggression, and of the victory of alien forces over the vulnerable self of the protagonist. It is not a struggle to the death, however, as in the gladiatorial games of "Todos los fuegos el fuego." This game has to do with the self's struggle to hold on to its own autonomy. The axolotl is possessed of enormous power of will, yet it wills to control through its own immobility. It is its stillness that first fascinates the man. Vaguely he understands that the purpose of its immobility is to abolish space and time. Yet through its "blind look" also comes the cry for help, "Sálvanos, sálvanos," which conjures up murmurings of consolation from the man. The sense of the animal's overwhelming power and enmity comes from the narrator's association of the axolotls with the ancient Aztecs. "Detrás de esas caras aztecas, inexpresivas y sin embargo de una crueldad implacable, ¿qué imagen esperaba su hora?" (Behind those Aztec faces, inexpressive and yet implacably cruel, what image was biding its time?) ("Axolotl," 127) The axolotls' objective reveals itself as another paradox. On the one hand, like the savage eruption of Aztec revenge in "La noche boca arriba," the axolotls hope to wreak vengeance and to escape their miserable, narrow cage. On the other, they cry out for help, they draw the man into their world, and they hope he will write about them to communicate their plight.

The dimension of time, then, works itself out in two ways in the story. The axolotl says that they feel time less if they remain quiet. This indicates that though these creatures inhabit time, they aspire to an existence in which time is nullified, an existence in the plane of the ideal. Historical time, the past, however, seems to fill them, even if one cannot attribute memory to them, and we have the sense that these ancient creatures occupy an intermediate, nebulous time between epochs of glory. Their victory over the man, their conquest of his self, is, however, only partial, for in some way he still exists outside of the axolotl. The most that the axolotls can hope to gain from their triumph is a story written about them. And that may be a vain hope, for the man is clearly losing interest in the axolotls at the end of the story. Indeed, what he has left behind is a moment of consciousness, his obsession: "Pero los puentes están cortados entre él y yo, porque lo que era su obsesión es ahora un axolotl, ajeno a su vida de hombre" (But the bridges are cut between him and me because what was his obsession is now an axolotl, alien to his life as a man) ("Axolotl," 130).

The epigraph to this chapter, "Para mí escribir forma parte del mundo lúdico,"[11] suggests the fundamental relation between game, the act and art of fiction, and metamorphosis in "Axolotl." Fictive creation sensed as play, as game, as ceremony, and as rite, however, takes on specific ontological and aesthetic dimensions in Cortázar's thought. The connection is elucidated in Cortázar's article "Para una poética," in which he develops a theory of art as analogy and compares the poet to the primitive magician (see the Introduction to this book).[12] The poet's use of image operates at the ontological level, that is, it has to do with the search for, and definition of, being.

El ciervo es un viento oscuro. . . . Al eliminar el "como" (puentecito de condescendencia, metáfora para la inteligencia), los poetas no perpetran audacia alguna; expresan *simplemente* el sentimiento de un salto en el ser, una irrupción en otro ser, en otra forma del ser: una participación. Pues lo que el poeta alcanza a expresar con las imágenes es *trasposición poética de su angustia personal de enajenamiento*. Y con nuestra primera pregunta: ¿Por qué es la imagen instrumento poético por excelencia?, enlaza ahora una segunda de mayor importancia: ¿Por qué ansía el poeta ser en otra cosa, ser otra cosa? El ciervo es un viento oscuro; el poeta, en su ansiedad, parece ese ciervo salido de sí mismo (y con todo siempre ciervo) que asume la esencia del oscuro viento. Paradójicamente podríamos emplear a nuestro turno la analogía y sostener que también el poeta (hacedor de intercambios ontológicos) debe cumplir la forma mágica del principio de identidad y *ser otra cosa*. . . .

(The deer is a dark wind. . . . When they eliminate the "like" [a little bridge of condescension, metaphor for the intelligence], poets are not being audacious at all; they are expressing *simply* the feeling of a leap of being, an eruption into another being, into another form of being: a participation. What the poet manages to express with images is *the poetic transposition of his personal anguish of alienation*. And to our first question—Why is the image the poetic instrument par excellence?—is joined now a second of greater importance: Why does the poet long to be in something else, to be something else? The deer is a dark wind; the poet, in his longing, is like that deer which has abandoned his self [and yet is still a deer] and which assumes the essence of the dark wind. Paradoxically we could use in our turn the analogy and argue that the poet too [maker of ontological interchanges] should carry out the magical form of the identity principle and *become the other thing*. . . .) ("Para una poetica," 131)

Poetry is the exploration of reality by way of analogy and is characterized by the capacity to admire. "Queda—trasladada a un plano metafísico, ontológico—la ansiedad de poderío" (There remains—transported to the metaphysical, ontological plane—the longing for power) ("Para una poetica," 133). Furthermore, this longing is inherited from our remotest ancestors. "En todo objeto—que el mago busca apropiarse *como tal*—el poeta ve una esencia distinta de la suya, y cuya posesión lo enriquecerá ontológicamente. Se es más rico de ser cuando, además de ciervo, se alcanza a ingresar en el viento oscuro. . . ." (In every object—that the magician tries to appropriate *as such*—the poet sees an essence distinct from his own and whose possession will enrich him ontologically. One's being is richer when, in addition to being a deer, one is able to form a part of the dark wind. . . .) ("Para una poetica," 133). Later he adds: "En las formas absolutas del acto poético, el conocimiento como tal (sujeto cognoscente y objeto conocido) es superado por la directa fusión de esencias: el poeta es lo que ansía ser. (Dicho en términos de obra: el poeta es su canto)" (In the absolute forms of the poetic act, knowledge as such [subject knower and object known] is transcended by the direct fusion of essences: the poet is what he longs to be. [Expressed in generic terms, the poet is his song]) ("Para una poetica," 137).

If we set the article "Para una poética" next to "Axolotl," the story reveals itself as an allegory of the act of writing (or the attempted act), and the axolotl is the vehicle for a double tenor: the *sujet*, the idea of the work as it forms itself within the writer, and also the completed work.[13] In the first function, as *sujet*, the axolotl dramatically calls itself to the writer's attention. The writer investigates it, contemplates it, becomes obsessed with it, becomes it. The complex characteristics of the animal which is *not* an animal suggest the nature of art itself for Cortázar. It belongs to the ancient past, embodying the primordial characteristics of its own nationality. (Although it lives in Paris, the axolotl is essentially, indeed quintessentially, Mexican.) Its surface remains material and specific, yet its essence is both illusive and allusive, drawing one into its mystery yet dispersing being into a shower of otherness. Lifeless and inanimate, yet breathing, it both absorbs and gives off life.

But what can we make of its anger and aggression? Roman Ingarden, in his phenomenological investigation of the being of the work of art, arrives at the conclusion that the sentence, like the literary work of art (of which it is the constitutive base), is a purely intentional object; that is, it is created through the intention of the writer. Yet the work would not be communicable or comprehensible if it did not have reference to ideal essences. Thus the sentence (read work of art) is neither a real nor an ideal object; it is "ontically heteronomous," that is, it belongs to both realms simultaneously.[14] Clearly, Cortázar would not agree with Ingarden in regard to the writer's intention. Like the unexplained metamorphosis of Gregor Samsa, like Cortázar's own protagonist's compulsion to vomit rabbits, or like the house invaded by a tiger, the *sujet* erupts within the artist mysteriously, absurdly, and penetrates his being. But once it takes control of him and he becomes it, he takes what he wants of its experience and then moves on. The work is left pleading for attention, somehow unengaged. Yet Cortázar's depiction does coincide with Ingarden's formulation of the work as both real and ideal. The axolotls inhabit time and yet make it stand still. They are both substance and essence. They are themselves and yet partake of a generalized otherness, approximating the mineral, the vegetable, the cultural object. And by inhabiting both the real and the ideal, they exist as points of transition and transfer. Like many of Cortázar's other protagonists, the nameless narrator of "Axolotl" is in search of his own being. For a while he both finds it and loses it as he merges with the axolotl/work of art. But he cannot finally find his "self" there because, like the game, the realm of the ideal in which the axolotl is partially poised can neither sustain life nor impede it. The game in "Axolotl" plays itself out and is abandoned. What is left is the artist's temporary obsession, the game board (hopscotch grid or sacred zone)/axolotl, ready to be engaged again (by a reader, a viewer), but never so intensely.[15]

Thus, metamorphosis in "Axolotl" takes on an explicit and direct relation to the act of writing, whereas the relation had been obscured in the works by Carpentier, Asturias, and Andrade. We discern an even clearer break between this story and the earlier narratives by the concentration in "Axolotl" on the individual in social isolation, on the individual in a lonely struggle for autonomy. In *Zona sagrada* we will confront metamorphosis as game and madness, enacted as individual pathology yet with significant social implications.

6 Metamorphosis as Revenge
Zona sagrada

In his interview with Luis Harss, Carlos Fuentes places the origins of the novel in social alienation:

"Because it's evident," says Fuentes, "that the novel as such was born as a form of opposition, of rebellion on the part of the writer, on the part of life itself, as expressed by the writer, against the rigidity of social patterns. In other words, without alienation there would be no novelist. Alienation is at the source of the novel. . . ."[1]

In the face of such a statement, one may ask what the novelist tries to achieve by the subsumption of myth (surely not a form deriving from alienation) into the fabric of the novel. *Zona sagrada* incorporates the myth of Ulysses into the structure of the novel, and yet, unlike Joyce, Fuentes holds the myth up to a refracted light in such a way that the meaning of the myth breaks into myriad negative possibilities. And Fuentes exploits the potential of myth for revealing a people's deepest fears and its despair. The bridge between the novel's chronicling of modern life (in the case of this novel, urban life) and myth's archetypal vision of the individual in his/her relationship to the cosmos is for Fuentes ritual or game. Just as art for Cortázar functions on an intermediate plane between life and the ideal, ritual/game for Fuentes provides the intermediate zone where the transcendental meets the mundane, where mind is dislocated by matter, where order and stasis are threatened, where myth dissolves into primeval/modern chaos.

In the opening scene of *Zona sagrada* Mito, the narrator, and Giancarlo, his schoolmate/lover/alter ego/spiritual twin, are in Positano, near the islands of the sirens who called to Ulysses, watching a soccer game. Giancarlo asks Mito how the myth of Ulysses ends, and Mito replies that Ulysses always returns, he always kills the pretenders, Penelope stops weaving forever, Telemachus always becomes again part of the household. A little later Giancarlo begins the retelling of the myth, which forms one of the essential designs in the fabric of the novel. The sirens did not sing as Ulysses passed; he said that he listened and resisted, but he lied. He passed in safety.

. . . el canto de las sirenas que sólo es escuchado por quienes ya no viajan, ya no se esfuerzan, se han agotado, quieren permanecer transfigurados en un solo lugar que los contiene a todos.

(. . . the song of the sirens, which is only heard by those who do not journey, who no longer exert themselves, who have been exhausted, who want to remain, transfigured, in one place that contains everyone.)[2]

The soccer game breaks the boundaries of the sacred zone (here, the playing field) and turns into a fistfight. And at the end of the sequence a horse carrying a blonde girl gallops out of the grottos. Her hair and the horse's mane, as though blended because they are of the same color, fly in the wind. She looks back at the sirens' isle. She comes from Amalfi, the caverns of Neptune. This opening sequence introduces many of the novel's significant motifs: the game defiled, the sacred zone overrun, the decadent version of myth,[3] the longing for what Fuentes calls "transfiguration," mythical doubling, the ball game (the game played by the divine twins, Hunahpú and Xbalanqué, in the *Popol Vuh*), the dream of the ideal melding of two beings into a freeing oneness (in the figure of the girl on the horse), and incest (Amalfi, a probable reference to Webster's incestuous tragedy).

In the next chapter we are introduced to Claudia, Mito's mother, who controls Mito absolutely by tantalizing him sexually and then rejecting him and by supporting him (or withdrawing support) economically. Claudia surrounds herself with an entourage of beautiful, ambitious young women and is always accompanied by her efficient, mannish secretary, Ruth. Claudia's obsession is to endure, to obliterate the past and the future. As Ruth says of her: "No nombra las cosas que pasaron, nunca. Son parte de lo que ella es, ahorita. No le creas si te habla de algo que ya pasó. Es un cuento que acaba de inventar; es parte de su presente" (She does not name things that happened, ever. They are part of what she is, right now. Don't believe her if she speaks of something that already happened. It's a story she invented; it's part of her present) (*Zona*, 109).

Zona sagrada incorporates layers of mythical underpinnings into the history of the hapless Mito and his fabled mother. Prominently displayed are the various decadent versions of the Ulysses story. Claudia is explicitly associated not only with Penelope and Circe, but also with the Llorona, the China Poblana, the Virgin of Guadalupe (Mexico's matron saint), the Medusa, Justine, Dragon Lady, Manta Religiosa, "Bella Dame san Mercy," Pussy Galore, Yahweh and Lucifer, Gaea and a Eumenide. Perhaps her most important symbolic function is suggested by her remark, "antes la imagen de México era Pancho Villa y ahora soy yo" (before the image of Mexico was Pancho Villa and now it is I) (*Zona*, 33). Beneath the layers of European myth mixed with "pop" image converge strands of the most basic of the mythical references, which are autochthonous, indigenous to Mexico, and which reveal themselves as contemporary social comment. Gloria

Durán, in *La magia y las brujas en la obra de Carlos Fuentes*, makes explicit this most fundamental function of Claudia: "Ella, como hemos visto, matriz, madre, tierra, México en símbolo y de hecho. . . ." (She, as we have seen, womb, mother, earth, Mexico as symbol and in fact. . . .).[4] Indeed, she is the incarnation of the Aztec goddess Coatlicue. Now Coatlicue is the mother of the gods, the sun, the moon, the stars, and is also the earth in its function as creator and destroyer. Antonio Caso describes the famous statue of her in the Museo Nacional as follows:

Lleva una falda formada por serpientes entrelazadas, de acuerdo con su nombre, sostenida por otra serpiente a manera de cinturón. Un collar de manos y corazones, rematando en un cráneo humano, oculta en parte el pecho de la diosa. Sus pies y sus manos están armados de garras, porque es la deidad insaciable, que se alimenta con los cadáveres de los hombres, por eso se llama también "la comedora de inmundicias". Pero sus pechos cuelgan exhaustos porque ha amamantado a los dioses y a los hombres, porque todos ellos son sus hijos, y por eso se la llama "nuestra madre" Tonantzín. De la cabeza cortada salen dos corrientes de sangre, en forma de serpientes representadas de perfil, pero que al juntar sus fauces, forman un rostro fantástico. Por detrás le cuelga el adorno de tiras de cuero rojo, rematadas por caracoles, que es el atributo ordinario de los dioses de la tierra.

(She wears a skirt formed of interwoven serpents in accordance with her name, sustained by another serpent in the manner of a belt. A necklace of hands and hearts, terminating in a human skull, hides in part the chest of the goddess. Her feet and hands are armed with claws because she is the insatiable deity that feeds on the cadavers of men and thus is called also the "eater of filth." But her breasts hang exhausted because she has nursed the gods and men, for all are her sons, and thus she is called "our mother" Tonantzín. From her severed head flow currents of blood, in the form of serpents represented in profile, but as the streams converge, they form a fantastic face. On her back hangs the ornament of red leather darts ending in snails, which is the ordinary attribute of the earth gods.)[5]

In a sophisticated interpretation of mythological symbolism in *Zona sagrada* (and also in *La muerte de Artemio Cruz* and *Cambio de piel*), Liliana Befumo Boschi and Elisa Calabrese point out that the metamorphosis of Mito is related to the transformation of Quetzalcóatl, the plumed serpent, into Xólotl, who is Quetzalcóatl in his humiliated form, forced to suffer wounds and insults in the other world and wearing the face of a dog.[6]

The metamorphosis of Mito, however, and mutability itself, which is the central theme of this novel, involve all of the levels of meaning and inform the very structure of the work. In order to elucidate the structure and the functioning of mutability in *Zona sagrada*, it will be helpful to focus on (1) the images of Baroque and *fin de siècle* decadence; (2) works of art, which in this novel are the paradoxical vehicles of stilled movement or dynamic stasis; and (3) the concept of transfiguration as extratemporal phenomenon.

The choice of Mexico City and Campania as the major axis points in the novel establishes Mexico City as the heir to the Baroque essence of the Italy of the late Renaissance. Mito moves from Guadalajara to Mexico City to Lausanne to Campania, back to Mexico, eventually back to Italy, to Paris, and finally back to Mexico, whereas Claudia, the novel's matrix/womb, inhabits only Mexico City and Campania. In the second of his important formative experiences, Mito is diverted, by Giancarlo's unseen hand, from his perusal of *Great Expectations* (in an ancient bookstore in Lausanne) to a collection of Villon, thereby being thrown forever off the track of Pip's journey toward optimistic wisdom and onto the path toward decadence and despair. He reads "Mais où sont elles, les neiges d'antan?" (But where are they, the snows of yesteryear?) and subsequently accepts Giancarlo's invitation into the Baroque labyrinth, the palazzo at Madonna dei Monti. Italian scenes always recall Mexico to Mito.

Madonna dei Monti asciende desde los valles brumosos de la Campania invernal hacia el conglomerado de plazas y calles rectas que tanto me recuerdan las de algunas poblaciones mexicanas; Orizaba, sobre todo, por la llovizna constante, la cercanía de la montaña, los balcones con barrotes de madera pintada. Pero, en seguida, la traza de ajedrez se pierde en el enjambre de callejuelas que han sido escalones, escalones que se convierten en pasajes, pasajes que serán túneles.

(Madonna dei Monti ascends from the misty valleys of wintry Campania toward the conglomeration of plazas and straight roads which remind me so much of those in some Mexican villages; Orizaba, above all, through the constant drizzle, the proximity of the mountain, the balconies with bars of painted wood. But, immediately, the chess board loses itself in the multitude of alleyways which have been stairs, stairs which become passageways, passageways which will be tunnels.) (*Zona*, 75)

Me detengo frente al palacio de Iturbide, donde está la tienda de modas; recuerdo la casa de Guadalajara. La piedra labrada del barroco, la floración excesiva que es la contra-consagración de nuestro miedo disfrazado de buen gusto, reticencia, medio tono; otra venganza, otro chantaje, el de los estilos pendulares de nuestra arquitectura y nuestras vidas.

(I stop in front of the Iturbide Palace where the fashion shop is; I remember the house in Guadalajara. The polished stone of the Baroque, the excessive flourishing that is the counter-consecration of our fear disguised as good taste, reticence, modulation; another revenge, another blackmail, that of the oscillating styles of our architecture and of our lives.) (*Zona*, 80)

The memory of the corrupted chaos of the palace reestablishes itself in the decor of the adult Mito's apartment in Mexico City. The long and convoluted Carpentier-like description of the apartment includes the following:

Ha crecido como una selva . . . mi continuidad está aquí y agradezco la fatiga fría, el sudor nervioso que me obliga a detenerme en el umbral y sentirme un objeto más, devorado por los extremos de la línea liberada: sierpes de todas las paredes cubiertas de seda escarlata: allí se trenzan las líneas puras y libres que encuentran todas sus combinaciones, todas sus conjunciones, todas sus fusiones. Hay una violación que libera cuando se encuentran dos extremos lineales, sin origen ni fin: nudos desatados, paralelas anudadas, pistilos delgados y quebradizos de vidrio opaco, lámparas de gotas de emplomado que son flores cerradas y frutas abiertas, . . . barrotes como rosarios entre la sala y el corredor, biombos de cisnes y danzarinas flacas, de costillar visible entre un espacio y otro de mi apartamento.

(It has grown like a jungle . . . my continuity is here and I am grateful for the cold fatigue, the nervous sweat which forces me to stop on the threshold and feel myself one more object, devoured by the extremes of the liberated line: serpentinings over all the walls covered with scarlet silk: there the pure, free lines which encounter all other combinations, all of their conjunctions, all of their fusions, twist around each other. There is a violation that liberates when the extremities of two lines, without origin or end, meet: knots undone, parallels joined, slender pistils and fragments of opaque glass, lamps of drops of leaded glass which are closed flowers and open fruit, . . . bars like rosaries between the living room and the hall, screens with swans and skinny dancers, like a visible ribcage between one space and another in my apartment.) (*Zona*, 30–31)

The description ends: "La zona sagrada me aísla y me continúa: afuera queda lo profano" (The sacred zone isolates and continues me: the profane stays outside).

It is Giancarlo again who has taught Mito the lesson of the proliferation of materiality:

. . . tú siempre insistías en describir y redescribir como la única burla posible que nos queda: los inventarios, los catálogos son la ironía final con la que se puede contestar a todas las historias gastadas, a todos los personajes vencidos, a todos los significados vacíos. Los objetos, que son el reino de las apariencias, se vengan del mundo impalpable, espiritual, que antes nos sojuzgó.

(. . . you always insisted on describing and redescribing as though it were the only possible way of ridiculing left to us: inventories, catalogs are the final ironies with which one can answer all the wasted histories, the personages conquered, the meanings emptied. Objects, which are the kingdoms of appearances, take revenge on the impalpable, spiritual world which before had us subjugated.) (*Zona*, 67–68)

Mito, then, finds his place in, indeed belongs irremediably to, an atmosphere of pure and profuse materiality. As we shall see, the question of materiality is central to the meaning of Mito's metamorphosis and to the whole complex of meanings that it brings together, resolves, and propels forward.

Specific works of art form a focus for the dialectic between, and interplay of, stasis and mutability in *Zona sagrada*. In the second chapter, in which Mito first attempts to describe his mother, he sees her as the subject of a triptych by Leonora Carrington—one of Carrington's works depicting a metamorphosis in process—a figure that "sabe conservar su rostro famoso y convertir su cuerpo en una perpetua metamorfosis de ave y ceniza, de llama y dragón" (knows how to preserve her famous face and convert her body into perpetual metamorphosis of bird and cinder, flame and dragon) (*Zona*, 12). Later Claudia describes the spectacle of Oberammergau as something that constantly repeats itself and yet in which nothing is repeated. You know how it is going to come out, she explains, yet you do not. It does not make you cry, but it changes you. Just before the first of his phantasmagoric experiences (the ritual performed by the *Erinias*), Mito analyzes two other of his mother's paintings, and here Baroque mutability emerges in its role as social comment. A painting of a pink and malign Gioconda by Botero faces a portrait by José Luis Cuevas of the Marquis de Sade. Both paintings stress "la corrupción hogareña" (domestic corruption), not just the decadence of bourgeois culture but also the poverty of bourgeois ideals. In addition, the portrait of Sade resists light, the light that we associate with living things. Finally, as the rite performed by the *Erinias* is about to take place Mito and the women turn again to the Carrington triptych:

Todos miramos hacia el tríptico de Leonora Carrington en el muro al fondo del salón. Es un retablo llevado al altar que era su destino: un cementerio abierto, de nardos y sauces llorones, se extiende detrás de Claudia y no sé si el cementerio real es el jardín desde donde nos observa la verdadera Claudia, si la falsa Claudia del jardín es la verdadera Claudia del retablo, la Claudia de la piel negra y las alas de murciélago. No sé cuál de las dos es la cabeza del can famélico que conoce cuanto lo rodea: los hombres vivos que podrían ser, al filo de la navaja, leones y lobos.

(We all looked toward the triptych of Leonora Carrington on the wall at the end of the room. It is an icon carried to the altar which was its destiny: an open cemetery, with spikenards and weeping willows, extends behind Claudia, and I don't know if the real cemetery is the garden from which the real Claudia watches us, if the false Claudia of the garden is the real Claudia of the painting, the Claudia of black skin and bat's wings. I don't know which of the two is the head of the hungry dog which is familiar with everything around it: the living men who could become, at the razor's edge, lions and wolves.) (*Zona*, 121–22)

Here, beyond the suggestion of metamorphosis and dynamism, beyond the operations of decay, mutability manifests itself in its most ominous function: that of casting doubt on the very perception of reality.

Like Claudia, Giancarlo fears and is obsessed with time. If Claudia creates an eternal present, Giancarlo seeks what he calls transfiguration, which is the negation of evolutive time, time in which events develop or unravel in a natural succession. Transfiguration achieves a leap into another state of being. As Giancarlo says: ". . . si te captura el tiempo te mata. Empieza, se desarrolla, termina. Si te transfiguras, sólo pasas de un estado a otro, siempre, incandescente, como las estatuas del palacio" (. . . if time captures you, it kills you. It begins, it develops, it ends. If you transfigure yourself, you only pass from one state of being to another, always, incandescent, like the statues of the palace) (*Zona*, 106). Transfiguration is the battle of the will against the inevitable consequences of what any given moment will bring. In the opening sequence Giancarlo characterizes the song of the sirens as a test of Ulysses' power of transfiguration as well as of his vocation for permanence. The sirens are those who would break the natural order, which is that of the myth resolved, foreseen. ("Converted into ritual," interjects Mito; *Zona*, 5.) The natural order is for Ulysses to be prudent; if he were to be distracted by the song, he would be transfigured. Thus, paradoxically, the involuntary act of succumbing would constitute a superior act of will and transfiguration. Giancarlo tells Mito that he must listen to the sirens, but Mito cannot, for he is distracted by beauty, the game, life. Later in the novel, on the night that Bela comes to his apartment (this time as herself, not made up as Claudia), Mito attempts, or imagines attempting, a scene that would defy transfiguration. He remembers Giancarlo's having said that everything transfigures, nothing develops, and he tells Giancarlo, who is ever present in his mind, that he plans to develop a scene. It is a typical Hollywood seduction scene, but one that would culminate in coitus and death. At the same time, the pragmatic Bela is bluntly undressing. Mito mentally confronts the realistic outcome of this encounter: clothes on the floor, wrinkled underwear. And then he faces the basis of his sexual conflict: he wants to lose himself in her and at the same time find her unattainable. The magical, Italian Bela sings the song of the sirens, and Mito resists, not because he is distracted by beauty, games, or life, but because his own sexual compulsions take over and dominate his behavior, and these, of course, have been created by his mother. "Sólo hay transfiguraciones" (There are only transfigurations), concludes Mito the following morning.

Late in the novel Mito returns to his recollections of his first stay at Madonna dei Monti and the ride back in Giancarlo's car on treacherous mountain roads. Terrified, Mito begs Giancarlo to be careful, to slow down; Giancarlo answers paradoxically that he wants to endure. Mito tells him not to laugh, and Giancarlo replies that he does not laugh, he transfigures himself. Giancarlo must take risks in order to undergo transfiguration, whereas Mito exists in a transfigured state, unable to develop.

Claudia's and Giancarlo's obsessions with time and death, with immortality, then, form a contrast to Mito's obsession, which is to fuse with his mother, to love her, to reenter her womb, and to become her. All of these are an obsession with metamorphosis, and the key to the climax and end of the novel is precisely the analysis of the existential elements inherent in Mito's metamorphosis and of the metamorphic crisis that brings together the mythic themes, the psychological conflict, and the social implications that inevitably derive.

Mito's psychic dilemma approximates that of Goyo Yic in *Hombres de maíz*—although Mito's is posed in more radically subjective terms than is Goyo's—in that he craves union with the woman in order to achieve wholeness. Mito is only a partial person, a splintered self. Like the protagonist of *Cumpleaños* (which critics have argued forms a trilogy with *Aura* and *Zona sagrada*[7]), Mito's need to achieve oneness with his mother is basic to his very survival, as well as to his identity. One does not have an identity if it is not completed by others.

Pero puedo completarla. Éste es el único pensamiento que acompaña mi acción: la plenitud de este verano con Nuncia en el bosque me necesita a mí, actuante, para ser completo. Sin mí, sería un gigantesco vacío. Y yo, el hombre que actúa para que el verano, la mujer y el bosque sean la misma cosa conmigo, desaparezco poco a poco para unirme a ellos: dejo de ser yo para ser más yo, dejo de ser yo para ser ellos. Dejo de conocerme para ser uno.

(But I can complete her. This is the only thought that accompanies my action: the fullness of this summer with Nuncia in the woods needs me, the agent, to be complete. Without me, it would be a gigantic emptiness. And I, the man who acts so that the summer, the woman, and the woods will be the same thing as I, disappear gradually to unite in them: I stop being myself in order to be more myself; I stop being I to be them. I stop knowing myself so as to be one.)[8]

In addition, Mito needs Giancarlo. Frank Dauster has argued that Giancarlo does not really exist at all, that he is a figment of Mito's imagination.[9] This is perfectly plausible since Giancarlo clearly enacts adversarial, conflictual roles that enable Mito to stake out his own functions, that allow Mito to play out Giancarlo's eroticism and violence vicariously, and that also permit Mito to rationalize his own defeat at the hands of a more powerful, sadistic double. Giancarlo fills Mito's empty spaces. As described by Giancarlo in the opening sequence, Mito's longing for the sacred zone, like that of Ulysses, is for a realm that would contain everyone, and in a transfigured state. The ideal would be the union of all three—Claudia, Giancarlo, and Mito—in a blended, completed self.

Metamorphosis as Revenge   91

The metamorphosis of body allows Mito to shift the center of his pain from the psyche to the flesh. Fuentes' use of myth is deliberately inconsistent, allowing associations of one myth to flow freely into those of another. Thus, the body of the transformed Mito is that of a dog, not that of one of Circe's pigs: a novel transformed into modern urban myth requires a city-dwelling animal. The image of the faithful subordination of the domestic dog suits Mito, whose outstanding characteristic is his submissiveness. Mito has gone so far as to mutilate his own dogs, and after they are gone, they haunt his consciousness. They are pure carnal presence.

Chejov dice que al morir dejan de funcionar cinco de nuestros sentidos y empiezan a vivir otros noventa y cinco. Y uno de ellos me dice que no estoy solo en mi recámara. Que otras presencias husmean y palpitan en la oscuridad, alrededor de la cama, entre las cortinas: sólo un aura. Pero es olor a sangre seca y metálica. De cicatrices que no se cierran. De pelambre húmeda y erizada. De anos rojos. De patas negras.

(Chekhov says that when we die five of our senses stop functioning and ninety-five come to life. And one of them tells me that I am not alone in my room. That other presences sniff and pant in the darkness, around the bed, among the curtains: only a vulture. But it is the smell of dried, metallic blood. Of moist, stiffened hair. Of red anuses. Of blackened paws.) (*Zona*, 136)

As a dog, Mito will suffer the same kind of humiliation and pain at the hands of Jesús that he has meted out to his own pets. On the other hand, he may well attain the same power of haunting endurance in the minds of his betrayers, Claudia and Giancarlo, that his dogs have had. And the triumph may well be his after all.

In no other of the modalities of the self is the fragmentation of Mito's being so graphically exposed as in his modes of perception. Jarringly acute, the signals of his senses nevertheless always trigger an existential revolt. Nothing is as it should be for Mito, and his instinctive reaction is to substitute, to displace, this reality for another one. Even so, the other reality is even more acutely seen, heard, smelled, tasted, felt than the one that actually contains his presence, as we see for instance, in the passage quoted in the previous paragraph. On the affective level, Mito's desires center exclusively on his obsession with his mother, and this, of course, forces askew his powers of judgment as well. Mito cannot be said to be truly capable of self-reflection because any attempt to contemplate himself is blocked by his pain. Until his metamorphosis, he remains a prisoner of his neurosis.

Life's central conflict for Claudia and for Giancarlo is one of will against time. As we have seen, Claudia needs to deny both past and future, to inhabit an eternal present in order to preserve her beauty, her magnetism, and thus her power, whereas Giancarlo's transfigurations represent strategies for endurance. Clearly, the fear of the orderly passage of time is the fear of death. The Baroque decadence that permeates the pores of this novel only reminds the characters and us that everything is quickly coming to ruin. Mito, however, does not enter into this kind of conflict. He imposes his will on reality only in his mind, by imagining it other, and by trying to create or return to his sacred zones. Lanín Gyurko has pointed out his sadistic strategies: as a child he takes out his frustrations—caused by the abuse and ridicule suffered at the hands of his game-playing classmates—by torturing and mutilating insects.[10] We have already seen his sadistic treatment of his dogs, a strategy for getting back at Claudia, who had given them to him. The most perplexing question surrounding Mito's metamorphosis is whether or not it is voluntary, whether Claudia casts a spell over him or whether it is an inexplicable misfortune in the manner of Kafka's Gregor Samsa. Gloria Durán has argued that the metamorphosis is worked by the witch, Claudia/Circe.[11] The text neither confirms nor denies this hypothesis. On returning to Mexico Mito goes to Claudia's house, to her bedroom. He smells, feels, caresses, kisses her clothing which still retains her perfume. He sinks into her furs. He understands that she is allowing him to see himself as another person, as her. He has a vision of witch burnings, imagining himself as Claudia, the only witch to escape. He dresses himself in her things, from her underwear to her lipstick to her golden serpent bracelet. Then he imagines himself denouncing her as a witch, and as he does so he becomes a dog.

¿Qué les diré cuando la denuncie? ¿Qué, cuando la vea subir a la hoguera? ¿Que lo terrible es saber que la hechicera es inocente y que por eso es culpable? ¿Que no podríamos vivir sin ella y que no podemos vivir con ella? No. ¿Bastará mostrarme así, demostrar que soy ella, que ella usurpa mi identidad, que ella me ha convertido en esto que los espejos reflejan: este príncipe de burlas, en este muñeco embarrado de cosméticos, en este seco árbol de Navidad cuajado de bisuterías, en este perro famélico que ya no puede sostenerse sobre los tacones altos, gigantescos, zancos, y cae arañando el vidrio, cae con el cofre vacío entre las manos y con él rasga los espejos?
  Debe ser exterminada. Ni siquiera los jueces están a salvo. Ella los fascina en el acto de juzgar. El señor deja de distinguirse del siervo. Ambos desean el amor y merecen el consuelo.
  De bruces, contemplo al ratón que me contempla desde un tubo de cristal.

(What will I say to them when I denounce her? What, when I see her enter the bonfire? That the terrible part is knowing that the sorceress is innocent and for that reason she is guilty? That we couldn't live without her and we cannot live with her? No. Shouldn't it be enough to show myself like this, demonstrate that I am she, that she usurps my identity, that she has turned me into what the mirrors reflect: into this prince of fools, into this doll smeared with makeup, into this dried-out Christmas tree curdled with trinkets, into this hungry dog which can no longer support himself on these gigantic, stilt-like high heels, and falls, clawing at the glass, falls with the empty box in his hands and with it scratches the mirrors?

She should be exterminated. Not even the judges are safe. She fascinates them in the act of judging. The master cannot be distinguished from the servant. Both desire love and deserve compassion.

Face down I contemplate the mouse which contemplates me from a crystal tube.) (*Zona*, 186–87)

This metamorphosis is neither voluntary nor worked by Claudia; nor is it in the mode of Kafka. Like Ovid's Procne and Philomela, like Niobe, Mito becomes the animal that best emblematizes and projects his extreme psychic condition and state of being. After returning to his apartment, he suffers abuse and humiliation at the hands of Gudelia and her lover Jesús, and he watches them ruin the reels of his mother's films which he had treasured. He witnesses the destruction of his most comforting sacred zone, his apartment. Nevertheless, the advantage of his new state of being is that he can accept all of this with relative equanimity. He still cares and is anxious about the relationship between Giancarlo and his mother: he dreams that they might come and make love in front of him. But the most significant outcome of his metamorphosis is that it affords him the only possible opportunity for revenge and for victory over Giancarlo and Claudia.

Pero yo los venceré. No porque decida atraerlos a mí para aprovechar su abandono erótico y entonces saltar, morderles los rostros, clavarles mis incisivos en las yugulares, no. Sólo porque, hermanos, tardamos en abandonar el vientre de nuestra madre, aunque ella pujaba por parirnos: creíamos que salir de ella, abandonarla, era morir. Nueve meses es un siglo. Y él, ahora, en brazos de ella, no querrá abandonar la vida, querrá permanecer enterrado en ella y temerá la muerte como los dos, antes de nacer, temimos la vida.

Yo no.

Ésa es mi victoria. Un perro sabe morir sin sorpresa.

(But I will defeat them. Not because I would decide to attract them to me to take advantage of their erotic abandon and then jump, bite their faces, sink my incisors in their jugulars, no. Only because, brothers, we took a long time to abandon the womb of our mother, although she pushed hard to expel us: we believed that leaving her, abandoning her, was dying. Nine months is a century. And he, now, in her arms, will not want to abandon life, he will want to remain buried in her and will fear death, just as the two of us, before being born, feared life.

Not I.

That is my victory. A dog knows how to die without surprise.) (*Zona*, 190–91)

And here the novel ends.

Having delineated the existential resonances of the metamorphosis, we can now proceed to an analysis of the mythical and social strata in order to determine how all levels of meaning unite in the metamorphic crisis. The pair Guillermo and Giancarlo are associated with several archetypal sets of twins: Telemachus/Telegonus, Abel/Cain, Dionysus/Apollo, and as we have seen in Aztec mythology, Quetzalcóatl and Xólotl. The key to the transcendental meaning of the metamorphosis resides in the relationship between the latter two. Laurette Séjourné, in her investigation of Aztec thought and religion, shows that the advent of the cult of Quetzalcóatl is the beginning of religion for the ancient Mexicans. That is, this cult rejects the simple practice of magic in favor of a new conception of the human being as a duality consisting of spirit and body. The spiritual aspect makes possible a communion with the gods. (Quetzalcóatl himself, the plumed serpent, bears the image of the earthly, the serpent, and the heavenly, the bird.) Furthermore, it is Quetzalcóatl—in concert with Xólotl, his underworld other self—who creates man and woman. In this collaboration Quetzalcóatl symbolizes spirit, and Xólotl, the dog, is matter. After quoting one account from the codices of this underworld scene of creation, Séjourné comments:

But what is most remarkable about these narratives is the positive rôle they give to matter. It has been seen that if Venus must cross the earth to unite with the Sun, the King of Tollan [Quetzalcóatl] sets out on his liberating voyage only after having committed the carnal act. Also, Quetzalcóatl does not succeed in his terrifying mission to the Land of the Dead until he as [sic] assumed the form of a dog and thanks to the worms and bees: that is, with the help of creatures who have no consciousness. This shows that, far from being a useless element that is only troublesome to the spirit, matter is necessary because it is only by the reciprocal action of one upon the other that liberation is achieved.[12]

Furthermore, another account of the deeds of Xólotl reveals him as the god who refused to die, and Séjourné points to the "multifarious relations that can be established between spirit and matter."[13]

We have already seen that in *Zona sagrada* Mito is specifically identified with materiality. Mito's metamorphosis only further connects him with matter, with earthly things, with life, and above all, with survival. But how does Claudia fit into this spirit/matter rivalry, and what is her role in the mythical scheme? Coatlicue/Tlazotéotl belongs to a sequence later in the Mexican pantheon than does Quetzalcóatl, for she is the mother of Huitzilopochtli, whom the Aztecs, recent conquerors of the other Mexican peoples, exalted as their god of war. (The cult of Quetzalcóatl seems to have emerged some fifteen hundred years earlier in the Toltecan capital, Teotihuacán.) Claudia/Coatlicue/Gaea, however, has the aspect of a Saturnian figure, a primal goddess, belonging to an epoch of unharnessed, chaotic barbarism. She is also a witch, and in Séjourné's scheme would be part of an epoch that precedes religion, in which all movement and change is associated with natural forces and their manipulation by human beings. Thus, Fuentes posits—as, in a way, Asturias had also—the transition from matriarchy to the creation of true man. Under the matriarchy man cannot reach his potential (and here man is the only consideration, for Claudia has no daughter and the destiny of woman is not an issue in the novel), cannot act for himself, has no autonomy, no real self. It is left to the spirit/Giancarlo to wrestle and to attempt to subdue the malign maternal force, as he promises Guillermo that he will try to do.

In the chapter entitled "Los hijos de la Malinche" of *El laberinto de la soledad*, Octavio Paz poses the dilemma of the Mexican's heritage. Son of the raped and traitorous Malinche, the Mexican must ultimately despise that aspect of himself that belongs to the defeated Indian past and to his mother, "la Chingada" ("La Chingada es la Madre abierta, violada o burlada por la fuerza" [The Chingada is the mother opened up, violated and mocked by force][14]). Nevertheless, in an enigmatic passage Paz suggests that the aftermath of the conquest, which came at the apogee of the cults of Quetzalcóatl and Huitzilopochtli, produced a double tangent in the worship of female deities: both the cult of the Virgin and a return to the worship of ancient female divinities.

Este fenómeno de vuelta a la entraña materna, bien conocido de los psicólogos, es sin duda una de las causas determinantes de la rápida popularidad del culto a la Virgen. Ahora bien, las deidades indias eran diosas de fecundidad, ligadas a los ritmos cósmicos, los procesos de vegetación y los ritos agrarios. La Virgen católica es también una Madre (Guadalupe-Tonantzina la llaman aún algunos peregrinos indios) pero su atributo principal no es velar por la fertilidad de la tierra sino ser refugio de los desamparados. La situación ha cambiado: no se trata ya de asegurar las cosechas sino de encontrar un regazo. La Virgen es el consuelo de los pobres, el escudo de los débiles, el amparo de los oprimidos. En suma, es la Madre de los huérfanos. Todos los hombres nacimos desheredados y nuestra condición verdadera es la orfandad, pero esto es particularmente cierto para los indios y los pobres de México. El culto a la Virgen no sólo refleja la condición general de los hombres sino una situación histórica concreta, tanto en lo espiritual como en lo material. Y hay más: Madre universal, la Virgen es también la intermediaria, la mensajera entre el hombre desheredado y el poder desconocido, sin rostro: el Extraño.

(This phenomenon of returning to the womb, well known to psychologists, is undoubtedly one of the determining causes of the rapid popularity of the cult of the Virgin. Now, the Indian female deities were goddesses of fecundity, linked to cosmic rhythms, vegetation cycles, and agrarian rites. The Catholic Virgin is also a mother [Guadalupe-Tonantzina some Indian pilgrims still call her], but her main attribute is not to watch over the fertility of the land but to be the refuge of the helpless. The situation has changed: it is not a question of assuring the harvests but of finding a lap. The Virgin is the consolation of the poor, the shield of the weak, the support of the oppressed. In sum, she is the Mother of orphans. All men are born disinherited, and our true situation is orphanhood, but this is particularly true for the Indians and poor of Mexico. The cult of the Virgin not only reflects the general condition of men but also a concrete historical situation, as much in the spiritual realm as in the material. What is more, universal Mother, the Virgin is also the intermediary, the messenger between disinherited man and the unknown power, faceless, the Otherworldly.)[15]

In *Zona sagrada* Fuentes poses a reworking of Mexican mythical history. Claudia/Coatlicue reigns in place of la Malinche or the Virgin. The female principle holds sway ruthlessly, as both ultimate creator and destroyer. But her demise will engender the release of both the power of the masculine principle and matter. Mexican man's coming to the fullness of his identity requires the overthrow of matriarchal influence and the harmonious interaction of spirit and matter. But only by virtue of having had such a mother (instead of the passive Malinche or the only-once-fertile Virgin) can the Mexican free himself from his labyrinth and his solitude.

To answer the questions of how the myths of Ulysses relate to the Mexican myths and how Italy as axis point relates to the dilemma of modern Mexico, one must establish the parallels between the two bodies of myth and look to the particular image of Italy set forth in the novel. The so-called myth of Ulysses is primarily known to us through the vehicle of epic, and that places it in rational, literate Western tradition. Fuentes eschews the use of primordial European myth—Fraser's vegetation cults, for example—in favor of a "myth" known to us through the classics. Thus, the novelist brings together in the two bodies of myth the dual heritage of modern Mexico. Nevertheless, the variants of the Ulysses myth as presented in the novel set up the possibility of variants to Mexican myth as well. Why does Fuentes set part of the action in Italy, instead of in Spain? Spain could certainly afford a similar kind of Baroque atmosphere, necessary to the depiction of the dissolution of an epoch, but it could not convey the "dolce vita" image that Fuentes needs to paint the "pop" quality of modern, movieland life. In addition, Italy provides the geographic link between the sirens' island and Mito/Mexico.

Game and the sacred zone on which it is played are clearly archetypal in this novel and take the form of ritual. Mito's interactions in the sacred zones have to do with his attempting to come into communion with the mother-goddess and with his trying to create himself. His inability to play the game, to enact the ritual, and the dissolution into chaos of his sacred zones underscore his role as matter, as that which defies transcendance. The celebration

Metamorphosis as Revenge

of materiality in the novel serves only to deny the efficacy of ritual. Ritual belongs to the primal past of the Matriarch and of the Furies (which never become Eumenides here) and to the sex/death struggle that will take place between spirit, longing for transfiguration and stasis, and the dynamic Mother.

In the prologue to *El reino de este mundo*, as we have seen, Carpentier proposes that we reintegrate myth into the conception of history for the purposes of fomenting social revolution. And in the passage quoted at the beginning of this chapter, Fuentes seems to identify the very function and origin of the novel in terms of revolutionary goals. Nevertheless, as Andrés O. Avellaneda has pointed out, Fuentes' use of myth in *Zona sagrada* actually negates history altogether.

Los elementos de circularidad, recurrencia, permutabilidad, transformación, los diferentes estratos míticos, se multiplican como en un juego de espejos afirmando la igualdad de los polos principio-fin, anulándolos como entidades. *Zona sagrada* participa, en este sentido, de la idea sobre la temporalidad que el autor atribuyó a *Cambio de piel*: "Hay una historia paralizada. Hay una historia convertida en Estatua de la Historia, remitida a sí misma, regresada a sí misma. No hay progreso histórico, eso es lo que está diciendo un poco la novela: no hay escatología, hay puro presente perpetuo."

(The elements of circularity, recurrence, permutability, transformation, the different mythic strata, multiply as in a play of mirrors, affirming the equality of the poles beginning and end, nullifying them as entities. *Zona sagrada* partakes, in this sense, of the idea of time that the author attributed to *Cambio de piel*: "There is a history paralyzed. There is a history converted into a Statue of History, turned back upon itself, returned to itself. There is no historical progress; that is what the novel is saying, sort of: there is no eschatology, there is only pure, perpetual present.)[16]

Transfigured time is mythic time, movieland time. Mito lives it until his metamorphosis, and Giancarlo and Claudia continually contrive to enter it. Only the metamorphosis holds out the faint possibility of a return to the material and historical, but it is too fragile and ambiguous, too demeaning and desperate for the reader to comprehend as more than the most tenuous hope. From *El reino de este mundo* to *Zona sagrada* we come full circle from a robust conception of human potential seen through the framework of both myth and history to a denial of history and a nihilistic vision of renewals of human defeat, corruption, and impotence as derived from decadent versions of myth.

7 Conclusion

From the outset I have maintained that the frequent incidence of narrations of metamorphosis to animal form in seminal modern Latin American texts constitutes a phenomenon of significance in twentieth-century Latin American social, aesthetic, and existential thought. This essay has set out to examine metamorphosis from a phenomenological perspective because that mode of investigation equips the critic with an ontological and epistemological framework through which to examine existential and metaphysical problems related to world and self, to the writer and his/her art, to text and reader. For, following Harold Skulsky, I have demonstrated again that the literary treatment of metamorphosis explores what it means to be human, the primordial qualities of humanness, what is lost and what is gained in imagined transformations. Further, I have accepted the phenomenological thesis that a self exists always and only in the context of a world, and in the interests of denying an artificial dichotomy between form and content, I have described the structure of the narrative as the narrative world, that world that is the context of the literary character's self. Nevertheless, setting forth premises derived from metaphysical speculation in no way negates social, historical, psychological, or anthropological knowledge that occurs in the text; indeed, uncovering the ontological basis of a phenomenon only opens the way to other modes of interpreting its significance. Generally, the dramatic crisis of the metamorphosis itself brings all of the levels of meaning and all of the values of the text into high relief. Thus, each chapter in this book was divided into considerations of (1) the narrative world, (2) the self of the transforming character, and (3) the metamorphic crisis.

The study of the dynamic of metamorphosis in the narrative world raises questions ranging from what kind of generic impulse would allow such a bizarre, irrational occurrence, to what significance the metamorphosis may have within the context of the narrative. The first type of question wants to know if the narrative is "fantastic," and, if so, how to define "fantastic" and how to break it down into categories. In order to discuss the particular narratives analyzed in this essay, it was necessary to circumvent the concept of "fantastic" because some of these narratives take seriously the historical moment in which they are set and the historical consequences of the metamorphoses. Thus it was crucial to establish a term and concept that could treat metamorphosis as a magical or a mythical or a realistic phenomenon. Alejo Carpentier asks us to suspend disbelief not just as we read novels but also as we contemplate history. All of the Spanish American writers treated here ask us to believe in another reality, one that exists beyond the reach of the Western, rational mind. This other reality may not be a world of the playful imagination so much as a world of the unconscious or mythic mind. Consequently, in this essay the term *mutability* was adopted, and it served several purposes.

The concept of mutability, first of all, recalls the art critics' attempts to describe the movement and dynamism that is the essence of Baroque art. It is fitting to apply a Baroque term to many modern Latin American writers because they consciously exploit the modern possibilities and implications of their Baroque heritage. Second, *mutability* is a neutral term with regard to belief or disbelief. If we call an Indian legend "fantastic," we violate it with our arrogance. By talking about stories, novels, myths, and legends as "mutable worlds," we are able to remain neutral as to whether we believe or not and yet remain engaged in the meaning of these worlds. Third, the term *mutability* is able to capture the dynamic quality of the narrative world which is the context in which a metamorphosis takes place. This dynamism is an anti-realistic conception, completely atypical of the mainstream of several generations of novels that Magic Realism succeeds. The realistic/naturalistic novel, which predominates through the 1940s in Latin America, requires verisimilitude in setting and manners, psychological motivation of characters, logic and plausibility in plot construction. Nothing happens in this type of novel that is not planned for and that cannot be explained rationally. This is the opposite of the "mutable" world. Just as the realistic novel assures conformity and adherence to the evidence of our senses with regard to how things in our world function (even though it may cause us to question social systems), the novel that is a mutable narrative world throws us into conflict with our most basic ontological assumptions. (And *Don Quijote*, the first modern novel, belongs decisively to the second category.) Thus, the term *mutability*, in its implications both of startling transformations and of the illusoriness of reality, permits the examination of metamorphosis in terms of myth, magic, and Modernism while at the same time placing the narratives in the context of their roots as novels.

The description of mutability in the narrative world takes into account narrative time as process and also rhetorical figures themselves as they create a sense of illusion and instability. In Carpentier's *El reino de este mundo*, for example, two kinds of time form counterpoints to each other. The historical process of one event following as a consequence of another juxtaposes itself to magical/natural cycles in which change involves interactions and transformations from one realm of the natural world to another. At the same time, in this and other narratives, rhetorical figures, such as paradox, ambiguity, and hyperbole, create disequilibrium and uncertainty. Indeed, according to Cortázar, metaphor, the most essential figure of figurative language, embodies transformation and expresses the most fundamental human urge, which is to experience the being of otherness.

The metamorphosis to animal form must be imagined to effect profound changes in the radical essence of the self. By taking on the theme of metamorphosis, the modern serious writer forces him or herself to study fundamental structures of the self, their essential qualities and the implications for their alteration in undergoing the trauma of metamorphosis. This book has examined four aspects of the self in transformation: the body, which is the self concretized, its sign; perception, the self's mode of coming to know, reflect, and judge; will, which is motivation, power and its limits, and action; and finally, the self's own mode of living time, its memory, presence, and projection toward the future.

Metamorphosis severely alters the self's circumstance, that is, the self's relationship to, and mode of involvement in, its world. When Fuentes' Mito becomes a dog, he manages to shake himself loose from the straitjacket of his obsessions and his neurosis. Though in many ways restrictive, the experience of becoming a dog offers him a certain new maneuverability in the stifling relationship with his mother. The adjustment to his new physical being involves a new orientation to space, for he will now be confined to his apartment. It will be his new world. His concentration thus becomes focused primarily on what is present, and yet the destruction of the apartment that had before been his most sacred zone means little to him now because his values have also undergone transformation. Gone are the acute and paranoiac obsessions; and they are replaced by the desire simply to be fed regularly. In his reduced and narrowed situation, Mito's typical passivity, his tendency always to be acted upon by others, conforms to his new nature as a domesticated animal. In this sense he is now more himself than he was as a man. But it is his altered relationship to time that most surely reveals the radical change in circumstance, for now he has lost the anxiety of the future and, unlike his antagonists, can face aging and death dispassionately. That, he says, is his final victory. Thus, the metamorphosis generally alters the self in such a way as to allow us to see that self in a new light. More than an alter ego, more than the exposed hidden side of the self, the being in metamorphosis is the self explored at its roots and subjected to a new pattern of positive and/or negative potentialities.

I have insisted that the metamorphic crisis functions to bring together the values and the levels of meaning that form the text. The metamorphosis of Nicho Aquino in Asturias' *Hombres de maíz* is a particularly vivid example of how this happens because the structure of this long and complex novel is so opaque as to obscure any link between Nicho and earlier characters and

Conclusion

events. Nicho's metamorphosis clarifies, first of all, the symbolic level of meaning that is bound to the Quiché mythology of the *Popol Vuh*. For Nicho belongs—as do Fuentes' Mito, Andrade's Macunaíma, and Carpentier's Mackandal—to the folklore that informs the consciousness of the peoples evoked in the novel. Second, Nicho's experience makes plain the social values of the novel. I have demonstrated that his metamorphosis represents the beginning of the reversal of his people's misfortunes which were instigated by the betrayal of Tomás Machojón and the death of Gaspar Ilóm. Third, the view of time and history in the novel becomes apparent through his transformation, for it provides the occasion for the return of the magician/healer Venado-de-las-siete-rozas, who had seemed to have disappeared from the novel and yet turns out to be one of its prime movers. The advent of the Venado establishes continuity with the past (and thus operates in historical time) and also acts as the link with the other world.

Nicho's metamorphosis is the dramatic climax of the novel, because as he is changed we see through his eyes visions of the other world which are the fundamental, yet previously hidden, background for what is being narrated. In varying ways the same is true for all of the metamorphic crises studied here and perhaps for modern fictional metamorphoses in general.

Although this is not primarily a historical study, I have made reference to certain aspects of the treatment of metamorphosis in modern Latin American texts as particular to the twentieth century. The method I have set forth is applicable to the analysis of metamorphosis as literary event in any text, regardless of period or nationality. Indeed, I have used the method to study metamorphosis in Ovid, Apuleius, Kafka, Lautréamont, and others.[1] However, the fact that metamorphosis is such a frequent theme in modern Latin American texts is consistent with certain intellectual tendencies current to modern thought in general and to Latin American writing in particular. For example, and very obviously, the thematization of metamorphosis coincides with the modern coming to prominence of the field of anthropology, which has inspired specialists and nonspecialists alike to a fascination with, and a respect for, the cultures of so-called primitive peoples. Modern writers have found in the myths, legends, tales, and songs of the non-Western cultures the frequent and significant narration of metamorphoses, and since the phenomenon is so suggestive and so rich in implications they have employed it in a wide variety of contexts. Nevertheless, the folkloric source usually remains explicit, for the discovery of national and cultural roots is one of the many motives of modern narrations of metamorphosis.

In a historical essay on time in narrative, M. M. Bakhtin tells us that metamorphosis, from its folkloric origins, is bound up with themes of identity and conversely that the folkloric image of man is intimately involved in transformation and identity.[2] Undoubtedly, this holds true in the adaptation of folkloric themes of metamorphosis to modern novels in Latin America. As I have demonstrated, all of the narratives studied here relate explicitly to the quest for cultural identity. Through the use of a phenomenological method concerned especially with the impact on the self, I have argued that metamorphosis reveals the image, or ontology, of human being as well. Thus metamorphosis in modern Latin American narrative is involved in issues of existential, social, and individual identity.

Metamorphosis belongs also to the special preoccupation with the nature/culture dichotomy that has dominated Latin American literature and social thought since Romanticism. Appearing two years before *Doña Bárbara*, *Macunaíma*, as one example (or Horacio Quiroga's "Juan Darién," which belongs to the same decade, as another), poses that dichotomy, not as a conflict of opposites but rather by means of metamorphosis, which is transformation and combining. In the particularly illustrative example of *Macunaíma*, the culture hero of the Indian legends, who is really a phenomenon of nature and the one who effects changes in nature, confronts in the novel the culture of the modern Brazilian city. His mastery of the culture and the bitter results of his loss of innocence must conclude in defeat and a metamorphosis which signifies escape.

Even though metamorphosis transcends Magic Realism, occurring, as it does, in works that precede the advent of that movement, it nevertheless finds a natural and prominent place in fiction that constructs itself so frequently out of indigenous folklore. For it is the Magic Realists, finally, who declare that the indigenous cultures have more to offer us than their quaint, exotic, picturesque appearances, and who begin to delve into and to reveal the modes of constructing and perceiving the world that belong to non-Western mentalities.

This leads to what I have suggested is the metamorphosis of the writer him/herself, for the creation of a world view so fundamentally alien requires an extraordinary leap into otherness. That Latin American writers should be obsessed with the idea of change should surprise no one who is aware of the current social and political climate. That the fascination with change should express itself in the archetypal symbolism afforded by metamorphosis should surprise us only for a moment, for as dozens of modern Latin American narratives have shown, the figure of the human-become-animal reaches deep into the past and generates, for the future, visions of humanness that are infinitely rich in potential. Furthermore, the writer who creates the mutable narrative world, who imagines the transforming being, who dreams metamorphosis and thereby metamorphoses him/herself, finally invites us, the readers, to transform, to open ourselves to the possibilities of being and knowing that exist beyond ourselves.

Notes

Notes for Chapter 1: Introduction

1. Harold Skulsky, *Metamorphosis: The Mind in Exile*, p. 15.
2. Octavio Paz, "Arte Mágico," *Las peras del olmo*, which I will quote and discuss at further length in the second part of this Introduction.
3. Luis Leal, "El realismo mágico en la literatura hispanoamericana," pp. 230–35. In response to an article by Angel Flores, Leal argues that Magic Realism does not derive from Kafka. Quoting Borges, Leal points out that the principal element in Kafka's "The Metamorphosis" and other works is the invention of intolerable situations and that for Kafka's characters these situations are not magic but excruciating and unacceptable. Nor, for Leal, is Borges a Magic Realist, since the fundamental characteristic of his work is the creation of infinite hierarchies. Leal's relevant passage is as follows: "Ninguna de estas dos tendencias permea las obras de realismo mágico, donde lo principal no es la creación de seres o mundos imaginados, sino el descubrimiento de la misteriosa relación que existe entre el hombre y su circunstancia" (p. 233) (Neither of these two tendencies permeates the works of Magic Realism, where the principal thing is not the creation of imaginary beings or worlds but rather the discovery of the mysterious relationship that exists between man and his circumstance) (my translation).
4. "El realismo mágico echa sus raíces en el Ser pero lo hace describiéndolo como problemático" (Enrique Anderson Imbert, "El realismo mágico en la ficción hispanoamericana," *El realismo mágico y otros ensayos*, p. 19) (Magic Realism roots itself in Being, but it does so describing it as problematical) (my translation).
5. Alejo Carpentier, "Prólogo," *El reino de este mundo*. The passage to which I am referring is found on page 15. It will be quoted and discussed further in the second part of this Introduction.
6. "Realismo mágico y nueva novela latinoamericana; Consideraciones metodológicas e históricas," in Horanyi Matyas, ed., *Actas del Simposio Internacional de Estudios Hispánicos*, p. 355. The translation that follows is my own. Clearly, the whole thesis of my essay argues against Dessau's contention that the ontological conception of human being as fundamental to Magic Realism somehow gets lost after Carpentier's and Asturias' early works.
7. Maurice Natanson, *The Journeying Self: A Study in Philosophy and Social Role* (Reading, Mass.: Addison-Wesley, 1970), p. 2.
8. An example of this kind of reading is James E. Swearingen, *Reflexivity in "Tristram Shandy": An Essay in Phenomenological Criticism* (New Haven: Yale University Press, 1977).
9. See, for example, Gaston Bachelard, *The Poetics of Space*, trans. Maria Jolas (Boston: Beacon Press, 1969) or Georges Poulet, *Studies in Human Time*, trans. Elliott Coleman.
10. The classic text of reader response criticism is Roman Ingarden, *The Cognition of the Literary Work of Art*, English edition trans. Ruth Ann Crowley and Kenneth R. Olson (Evanston: Northwestern University Press, 1973). Wolfgang Iser and other reader response critics trace the origins of their method to Ingarden.
11. "Phenomenology is the study of essences; and according to it, all problems amount to finding definitions of essences; the essence of perception, or the essence of consciousness, for example. But phenomenology is also a philosophy which puts essences back into existence, and does not expect to arrive at an understanding of man and the world from any starting point other than that of their 'facticity' . . . but it also is a philosophy for which the world is always 'already there' before reflection begins—as an inalienable presence; and all its efforts are concentrated upon re-achieving a direct and primitive contact with the world, and endowing that contact with a philosophical status" (Maurice Merleau-Ponty, *Phenomenology of Perception*, trans. Colin Smith, p. vii).
12. "By a purely intentional objectivity we understand an objectivity that is in a figurative

sense "created" by an act of consciousness or by a manifold of acts . . ." (Roman Ingarden, *The Literary Work of Art: An Investigation on the Borderlines of Ontology, Logic, and Theory of Literature,* trans. George G. Grabowicz, p. 117).

13. Martin Heidegger, *Being and Time,* trans. John Macquarrie and Edward Robinson, p. 27. "Being-in is not a 'property' which Dasein sometimes has and sometimes does not have, and *without* which it could *be* just as well as it could with it. It is not the case that man 'is' and then has, by way of an extra, a relationship-of-Being towards the 'world'—a world with which he provides himself occasionally. Dasein is never 'proximally' an entity which is, so to speak, free from Being-in, but which sometimes has the inclination to take up a 'relationship' towards the world. Taking up relationships towards the world is possible only *because* Dasein, as Being-in-the-world, is as it is. This state of Being does not arise just because some other entity is present-at-hand outside of Dasein and meets up with it. Such an entity can 'meet up with' Dasein only in so far as it can, of its own accord, show itself within a *world*" (p. 84). And Edmund Husserl makes a similar point with regard to consciousness: "In the order pertaining to constitution of a world *alien to my ego*—a world *'external'* to *my own concrete Ego* (but not at all in the natural spatial sense)—that reduced world is the intrinsically first, the *'primordial' transcendency* (or 'world'); and, regardless of its *ideality* as a synthetic unity belonging to an infinite system of my potentialities, it is *still a determining part of my own concrete being,* the being that belongs to me as concrete ego" (Edmund Husserl, *Cartesian Meditations: An Introduction to Phenomenology,* trans. Dorion Cairns, p. 106).

14. Claude Lévi-Strauss, "L'Analyse morphologique des contes russes," p. 122. The translation is my own.

15. Heinrich Wölfflin, *Principles of Art History: The Problem of the Development of Style in Later Art,* 6th ed., trans. M. D. Hottinger, p. 14.

16. Tzvetan Todorov, *The Fantastic: A Structural Approach to a Literary Genre,* trans. Richard Howard.

17. Paul Ricoeur, *Freedom and Nature: The Voluntary and the Involuntary,* trans. Erazim V. Kohák, pp. 9–10.

18. Henry W. Johnstone, Jr., *The Problem of the Self,* pp. 9, 11.

19. Irving Massey, *The Gaping Pig: Literature and Metamorphosis.* For Massey, metamorphosis is an escape from public language: "It is a critique from the point where language has been forced on one" (p. 1).

20. Merleau-Ponty, *Phenomenology of Perception,* p. 82.

21. "Now the body is essentially an expressive space. If I want to take hold of an object, already, at a point of space about which I have been quite unmindful, this power of grasping constituted by my hand moves upwards towards the thing. I move my legs not as things in space two and a half feet from my head, but as a power of locomotion which extends my motor intention downwards. The main areas of my body are devoted to actions, and participate in their value, and asking why common sense makes the head the seat of thought raises the problem as asking how the organist distributes, through 'organ space', musical significances. But our body is not merely one expressive space among the rest, for that is simply the constituted body. It is the origin of the rest, expressive movement itself, that which causes them to begin to exist as things, under our hands and eyes" (Ibid., p. 146).

22. Skulsky makes reference to two of these animals, the bat and the whale, in his extraordinary first chapter, pp. 1–9. The reader is also referred to the definitive philosophical discussion of this question (to which Skulsky makes extensive reference): Thomas Nagel, "What is it like to be a Bat?" pp. 435–50.

23. Ricoeur, *Freedom and Nature,* p. 3.

24. I am here drawing on the outline of Ricoeur's study of the voluntary and the involuntary, in which the three main divisions are (1) decision and its motivations, (2) motion, and (3) consent, which is the surrender to determining factors.

25. Francis Fergusson, Introduction to *Aristotle's Poetics,* trans. S. H. Butcher, p. 8.

26. Poulet, *Studies in Human Time.*

27. A fascinating example is given by John N. Bleibtreu in *The Parable of the Beast.* In his opening chapter he describes the female cattle tick which lives the first part of its life lacking a pair of legs and sex organs and attacking only cold-blooded animals. After shedding its skin

several times, it enters a state of suspended animation which has been observed to last as long as eighteen years. The sperm she has received remains encapsuled during this dormant period. What she waits for is the scent of butyric acid, a substance present in the sweat of mammals. Bleibtreu comments: "The tick represents, in the conduct of its life, a kind of apotheosis of subjective time perception. For a period as long as eighteen years nothing happens. The period passes as a single moment; but at any moment within this span of literally senseless existence, when the animal becomes aware of the scent of butyric acid it is thrust into a perception of time, and other signals are suddenly perceived" (pp. 3-4).

28. Paz, "Arte mágico," pp. 184-85. The translation is my own.
29. Georges Poulet, "Phenomenology of Reading," p. 50.
30. Carpentier, "Prólogo," p. 9 (translations of this work are my own).
31. Ibid., pp. 10-11; 15-16.
32. Luis López Alvarez, *Conversaciones con Miguel Angel Asturias*, p. 168. The translation is my own.
33. Julio Cortázar, "Para una poética," pp. 121-38.

Notes for Chapter 2: Metamorphosis as Problematic Destiny

1. All references to "Los fugitivos" will be from Alejo Carpentier, *Cuentos completos*, pp. 115-49, and will be cited hereafter in the text as LF. The translations are my own.
2. Paul Ricoeur, *Freedom and Nature: The Voluntary and the Involuntary*, pp. 89, 99, 101.
3. Roberto González Echevarría, *Alejo Carpentier: The Pilgrim at Home*, pp. 131-35. For discussions of Carpentier as historical novelist, see also Emil Volek, "Análisis e interpretación de 'El reino de este mundo' de Alejo Carpentier," in Helmy F. Giacoman, ed., *Homenaje a Alejo Carpentier: Variaciones interpretativas en torno a su obra*; Roberto González Echevarría, "Historia y alegoría en la narrativa de Carpentier," pp. 200-220; and Ileana Rodríguez "Historia y alegoría en Alejo Carpentier," *Hispamérica* 17 (1977): pp. 24-45.
4. The cyclical pattern of historical events has been studied by Esther P. Mocega-González, "*El reino de este mundo* de Alejo Carpentier," pp. 219-39. González Echevarría interprets the cyclical pattern in terms of Carpentier's reading of Spengler, in *Pilgrim*, pp. 34-96.
5. Alejo Carpentier, *El reino de este mundo*, pp. 24-25, cited hereafter in the text as *El reino*. The English translation is taken from *The Kingdom of this World*, trans. Harriet de Onís (New York: Alfred Knopf, 1957), p. 4, cited hereafter in the text as *The Kingdom*.
6. Papá Legbá belongs to the first rank of Voodoo deities. According to Alfred Métraux, *Le Vaudou haïtien*, pp. 88-89, he is the first of the gods to be greeted in ceremonies. The guardian of doors and gates, he is the god who opens the way, not only in earthly pursuits but also to the heavens. In Dahomey Legbá is the interpreter of the gods, and without him the gods would not be able to communicate with men.
7. This statement actually occurs almost at the end of the novel, in part 4, chapter 3.
8. González Echevarría, *Pilgrim*, p. 205.
9. Especially by Mocega-González, "*El reino*," and by Juan Barroso, "*Realismo mágico*" *y* "*lo real maravilloso*" *en El reino de este mundo y El siglo de las luces* (Miami: Editores Universal, 1977), pp. 68-90.
10. "El maestro de Ti Noel, según el rasgo que le atribuye Carpentier, es una fusión del narrador popular haitiano, esencialmente dramático, y del *griot* africano, analista, moralista, poeta y educador de príncipes, que exalta el pasado de su nación para azuzar el orgullo y la valentía de sus discípulos" (Emma Susana Speratti-Piñero, "Noviciado y apoteosis de Ti Noel en 'El reino de este mundo,' " p. 205; more information and bibliographical references with regard to the Haitian storyteller and the *griot* are given in notes 15 and 16 on the same page) (Ti Noel's teacher, according to the traits that Carpentier attributes to him, is a fusion of the popular Haitian storyteller, essentially dramatic, and of the African *griot*, analyst, moralist, poet, and educator of princes, who exalts the past of his nation to stimulate the pride and courage of his disciples) (my translation).

11. The functions of the *mambo* and the *houngan* are described in detail in Métraux, *Le Vaudou*, pp. 53–59.

12. As a result of exhaustive research, Speratti-Piñero, "Noviciado y apoteosis," pp. 221–23, finds that the King of Angola is a *loa* who had been a powerful king on earth. Once a mortal has been possessed by a *loa*, he/she attains possible immortality.

13. Alejo Carpentier, *Tientos y diferencias*, p. 36. The translation is my own.

14. Alejo Carpentier, *El siglo de las luces*, cited hereafter in the text as *El siglo*. The translations that follow the passages quoted are my own.

15. González Echevarría, *Pilgrim*, p. 224.

16. González Echevarría, in *Pilgrim*, p. 133, quotes from Moreau de Saint-Méry, *Description topographique, physique, civile, politique et historique de la partie française de l'Isle de Saint Domingue* (Philadelphia, 1797), 2:630–31, as follows:

Le hasard ayant voulu que le poteau où l'on avait mis la chaine qui le saisissait fut pourri, les efforts violents que lui faisaient faire les tourments du feu, arrachèrent le piton et il culbuta par-dessus le bûcher. Les nègres crièrent: *Macandal sauvé*; la terreur fut extrême; toutes les portes furent fermées. Le détachement de Suisses qui gardait la place de l'exécution la fit évacuer; le geolier Massé voulait le tuer d'un coup d'épée, lorsque d'après l'ordre du Procureur-général, il fut lié sur une planche et lancé dans le feu. Quoique le corps de Macandal ait été incinéré, bien des nègres croyent, même à présent, qu'il à pas péri dans le supplice.

(Fate having decreed that the stake where they had put the chain that held him was rotten, the violent efforts that the torments of the fire caused him to make tore out the bolt, and he tumbled over the pyre. The Blacks cried: Mackandal is saved; the terror was extreme; all the gates were closed. The Swiss detachment that guarded the place of execution evacuated everyone; Massé, the jailer, wanted to kill him with the thrust of a sword, then, on the order of the attorney general, he was tied to a plank and thrust into the fire. Although Mackandal's body was incinerated, many Blacks believe, even now, that he did not perish in the execution) (my translation).

17. One of many examples is Ti Noel's comparison of African and European princeliness.

En el Africa, el rey era guerrero, cazador, juez y sacerdote; su simiente preciosa engrosaba, en centenares de vientres, una vigorosa estirpe de héroes. En Francia, en España, en cambio, el rey enviaba sus generales a combatir; era incompetente para dirimir litigios, se hacía regañar por cualquier fraile confesor, y, en cuanto a riñones, no pasaba de engendrar un príncipe debilucho, incapaz de acabar con un venado sin ayuda de sus monteros, al que designaban, con inconsciente ironía, por el nombre de un pez tan inofensivo y frívolo como era el delfín. Allá, en cambio—en *Gran Allá*—, había príncipes duros como el yunque, y príncipes que eran el leopardo, y príncipes que conocían el lenguaje de los árboles, y príncipes que mandaban sobre los cuatro puntos cardinales, dueños de la nube, de la semilla, del bronce y del fuego." (*El reino*, 28–29)

(In Africa the king was warrior, hunter, judge, and priest; his precious seed distended hundreds of bellies with a mighty strain of heroes. In France, in Spain, the king sent his generals to fight in his stead; he was incompetent to decide legal problems; he allowed himself to be scolded by any trumpery friar. And when it came to a question of virility, the best he could do was to engender some puling prince who could not bring down a deer without the help of stalkers, and who, with unconscious irony, bore the name of as harmless and silly a fish as the dolphin. Whereas Back There there were princes as hard as anvils, and princes who were leopards, and princes who knew the language of the forest, and princes who ruled the four points of the compass, lords of the clouds, of the seed, of bronze, of fire.) (*The Kingdom*, p. 8).

18. Métraux, *Le Vaudou*, p. 71, points out that the Haitians continually add new *loas* to the pantheon. Often the new *loas* are former heroes, kings, or revered members of the community. We have already seen that the King of Angola is such a case.

19. In a conversation I had with Adolf Snaidas, he pointed out that Carpentier sets Ti Noel up

for failure by having him choose a species, the goose, that is imported, not native to Haiti, and thus surely incompatible.

20. The "moment of vision" is a state of ecstasy in which Dasein encounters authentically and in a state of resoluteness that which has occurred, that which is present at hand, and the circumstances and possibilities that arise from past and present. It is "a coming-back to one's ownmost Self, which has been thrown into its individualization" (Martin Heidegger, *Being and Time*, pp. 387–88).

21. José Sánchez-Boudy, *La temática novelística de Alejo Carpentier*, p. 85. The translation is my own. On page 88, Sánchez-Boudy comments in passing that Carpentier's contacts with Heidegger's philosophy are unmistakable, although he does not specify. He is one of the few critics who have made any attempt to interpret the metamorphoses: "Las metamorfosis de Tío Noel son simbólicas. Quieren decir: el hombre puede ser lo que él desee. Puede crear. En otras palabras, crea sus valores" (p. 89 n. 15) (The metamorphoses of Tío Noel are symbolic. They mean that man can be whatever he desires. He can create. In other words, he creates his values) (my translation).

22. Speratti-Piñero, "Noviciado y apoteosis," pp. 226–28.

23. One of the principal offenders in this regard is Graciela Maturo in her article "Religiosidad y liberación en 'Ecué-Yamba-O' y 'El reino de este mundo,'" in *Historia y mito en la obra de Alejo Carpentier* (Buenos Aires: Fernando García Cambeiro, 1972), pp. 53–86.

24. Several critics have wished to interpret the "Ti" of "Ti Noel" as "Tío" (see for example the quotation in note 21, above). "Ti" in Haitian usage is a shortening of "petit."

Notes for Chapter 3: Metamorphosis as Integration

1. For example, Seymour Menton, *Historia crítica de la novela guatemalteca*, pp. 221–22, faults the novel for its lack of unity and attributes the problem to Asturias' attempt to break with the traditional concept of the novel. Giuseppe Bellini, *La narrativa de Miguel Angel Asturias*, trans. Ignacio Soriano, p. 69, concurs with Menton and finds that the last two chapters of the novel have only an artificial relationship to the preceding ones.

2. See for example, Luis Harss and Barbara Dohmann, *Into the Mainstream: Conversations with Latin American Writers*; Rita Guibert, *Seven Voices: Seven Latin American Writers Talk to Rita Guibert*, trans. Frances Partridge, pp. 121–79; and Luis López Alvarez, *Conversaciones con Miguel Angel Asturias*.

3. This is a summary of García's chapter 3, pp. 28–36.

4. Miguel Angel Asturias, *Hombres de maíz* (Buenos Aires: Editorial Losada, 1949), p. 20, cited hereafter in the text as *Hombres*. The translation is taken from *Men of Maize*, trans. Gerald Martin, p. 15, cited hereafter in the text as *Men*.

5. I have altered Martin's translation of "muñeco"—"scarecrow"—to "doll."

6. "At first they spoke, but their face was without expression; their feet and hands had no strength; they had no blood, nor substance, nor moisture, nor flesh; their cheeks were dry, their feet and hands were dry, and their flesh was yellow" (*Popol Vuh: The Sacred Book of the Ancient Quiché Maya*, trans. Delia Goetz and Sylvanus G. Morley, p. 89).

7. *Popol Vuh*, p. 93.

8. A typical passage from *Mulata de tal* is the following: "—Sola con su humo poblado de risas, ante las extrañas visiones de sueños de pesadilla reflejados en espejos donde tan pronto se ve uno gigante, como enano . . ." (p. 58) (—Alone, with her smoke populated by laughter, before the strange visions of nightmares reflected in mirrors where one sees oneself gigantic, like a dwarf . . .) (my translation).

9. Vera Popov Maligec attributes imagery of reflection and refraction in Asturias' work to the "strange Guatemalan light which, refracted on the waters of the many lakes and rivers, distorts the perspective making things appear distant, 'as if reflected in a mirror or through a lens or crystal'" ("Telluric Forces and Literary Creativity in Miguel Angel Asturias" [Ph.D. diss., Columbia University, 1976], p. 6).

10. According to García, *Hombres de maíz*, p. 44, dream coincides with the moment of creation.

11. As quoted in Harss and Dohmann, *Into the Mainstream*, p. 79.
12. For interpretations of color symbolism in Maya/Quiché belief, see Raphael Girard, *Esotericism of the Popol Vuh*, trans. Blair A. Moffett, pp. 140–41.
13. García, *Hombres de maíz*, p. 32.
14. Leo Spitzer, "Linguistic Perspectivism in the *Don Quijote*," *Linguistics and Literary History: Essays in Stylistics*, pp. 41–86.
15. "Canelo" suggests "cinnamon"; "jobo" denotes "wood."
16. The name is explained in the following passage: "Noche a noche, don Casualidón se repetía las palabras de San Remigio al bautizar al Rey Clodoveo, en la Catedral de Reims: 'Inclina la cabeza, fiero Sicambro, adora lo que tú has quemado y quema lo que hasta ahora habías adorado' " (*Hombres*, 240) ("Night after night Don Casualidón would repeat the words of Saint Remiguis as he baptized King Clovis in the cathedral at Rheims: 'Bow your head, proud Frank, worship what you have burned, and burn what you have worshipped' "; *Men*, 282).
17. *Popol Vuh*, p. 129.
18. The revelation of this connection is so significant that it occurs only in the last paragraph of the novel.

—¡María la Lluvia, la Piojosa Grande, la que echó a correr como agua que se despeña, huyendo de la muerte, la noche del último festín en el campamento del Gaspar Ilóm! ¡Llevaba a su espalda al hijo del invencible Gaspar y fué paralizada allí donde está, entre el cielo, la tierra y el vacío! ¡María la Lluvia, es la Lluvia! ¡La Piojosa Grande es la Lluvia! . . . (*Hombres*, 278)

(María the Rain, La Piojosa Grande, she took flight like cascading water, running from death, the night of the last feast in the camp of Gaspar Ilom! On her back she bore the son of the invincible Gaspar and was paralyzed there where she is, between the sky, the earth, and the void! María the Rain is the Rain! The Great Fleabag is the Rain!) (*Men*, 327)

19. In addition, Asturias maintains that among the present-day Indian population of Guatemala, "words capture the essence of things. To be able to put an exact name on something . . . means to reveal it, to bare it, to strip it of its mystery. 'That's why in the villages of Guatemala all the men answer to the name of Juan, all the women to the name of María. Nobody knows their real names. If a person knew the name of a man's wife, he could possess her, in other words, snatch her from her husband' " (As quoted in Harss and Dohmann, *Into the Mainstream*, p. 83). I am assured by Nathaniel Tarn, who has lived among the Indians of Guatemala, that this is untrue.
20. Girard, *Esotericism of the Popol Vuh*, p. 37.
21. Julian Pitt-Rivers, "Spiritual Power in Central America: The Naguals of Chiapas," in *Witchcraft Confessions and Accusations*, ed. Mary Douglas, p. 186; Benson Saler, *Nagual, brujo y hechicero en un pueblo quiché*, p. 8.
22. Daniel G. Brinton, *Nagualism: A Study in Native American Folk-lore and History*.
23. At least according to what one can gather from Pitt-Rivers' study of Chiapas, Brinton's of various areas of Mexico, or Lucille N. Kaplan's "*Tonal* and *Nagual* in Coastal Oaxaca, Mexico," pp. 363–68.
24. Brinton, *Nagualism*, pp. 15–19, elaborates considerably on the connection between the person's birth date, his/her nagual, and the name of the day according to the Maya calendar.
25. Girard, *Esotericism of the Popol Vuh*, p. 339.
26. Referring to the defeat of the four hundred boys by Zipacná in the *Popol Vuh*, Girard, *Esotericism of the Popol Vuh*, p. 76, states, "This legend, dramatizing the fatal consequences of drunkenness, illustrates another rule of native morality which prohibits excess in drinking liquor, limiting its use to a number of cups determined by ritual figures (four or five)."
27. Girard, *Esotericism of the Popol Vuh*, p. 60. Nathaniel Tarn has pointed out to me that Girard's interpretation of the four ages of the *Popol Vuh* in terms of the history of the Quiché has been discredited in recent years. However, there is considerable internal evidence to suggest that Asturias knew and accepted Girard's views.
28. The passage reads:

Sólo cuando oía hablar mujeres, acordaba Goyo Yic que andaba buscando a la María Tecún. Últimamente ya no pensaba mucho en ella. Pensaba, sí, pero no como antes, y no porque estuviera conforme, sino porque . . . no pensaba. ¡Ay, alma de tacuatzín! ¡Ay, ojos de tacuatzín! Era cobarde. El hombre es cobarde. Ahora, cuando pensaba en ella, al oír hablar mujeres, ya no le daba como antes un vuelco el corazón, y se estretenía [sic] en pensarla con un hombre rico. . . . ¿Para qué la iba a buscar él que si recobró los ojos, se le metió en el alma un tacuatzín? Los años, la pena que no ahorca con lazo, pero ahorca, los malos climas en que había estado durmiendo a la quien vive, en sus vueltas de achimero, registrando todos los pueblos y aldeas de la costa, y el paño de hígado en la cara de tanto beber aguardiente para alegrarse un poco el gusto amargo de la mujer ausente, lo fueron apocando y apocando, hasta darle la condición de uno que no era ninguno. Materialmente era alguien, pero moralmente no era nadie. Hacía las cosas porque tenía que hacerlas, no como antes, con el gusto de hacerlas para algo y fué peor cuando perdió la esperanza de encontrar a la mujer y a sus hijos. Hay tristezas que abrigan. La de Goyo Yic era tristeza de intemperie. (*Hombres*, 125)

(Only when he heard some women talking did Goyo Yic remember that he was looking for María Tecún. He hadn't been thinking about her so much lately. He thought about her all right, but not like before. This was not because he was resigned, but because . . . he just didn't. Soul of the possum! Eyes of the possum! He was a coward. Man is cowardly. Now, when he thought about her as he heard other women talking, it no longer made his heart miss a beat, and he amused himself imagining her with some rich man. . . . Why should he go looking for her, he who, though he had recovered his eyes, had a possum slipped into his soul? The years, the grief that doesn't hang you with a noose but hangs you just the same, all those nights he'd slept out in the open in bad weather on his peddling tours, searching through all the towns and villages along the coast, and the red liver blotches over his face from drinking so much liquor, to try and sweeten the bitter taste of his absent woman, little by little diminished him, until he was turned into someone who was no one. He did things because he had to do them, not like before, with the pleasure of doing them to some purpose, and it was still worse when he lost all hope of finding his woman and children. There are woes that shelter a man. Goyo Yic's was a rough weather woe.) (*Men*, 142–43)

29. This occurs before the first men, those of mud, were created (*Popol Vuh*, p. 85).
30. Ibid., pp. 90–92.
31. Girard, *Esotericism of the Popol Vuh*, p. 246.
32. Ibid., p. 262.
33. For example, Richard J. Callan finds embedded in the last chapter matter based on myths of Dionysus (Nicho Aquino's real name is Dionisio), Attis, Adonis, Persephone, Hermes, Isis, and Osiris ("The Quest Myth in Miguel Angel Asturias' *Hombres de maíz*," pp. 249–61).
34. See Girard, *Esotericism of the Popul Vuh*, p. 136.
35. During the third of the tests that the twins undergo in the underworld, they are required to gather flowers, but the flowers are closely guarded. The ants gather the flowers, thereby helping the twins to pass the test and avert death (*Popol Vuh*, pp. 146–47).
36. *El libro del consejo*, trans. Georges Raynaud, J. M. González de Mendoza, and Miguel Angel Asturias, pp. 187, 190; Robert M. Carmack, *The Quiché Mayas of Utatlán: The Evolution of a Highland Guatemalan Kingdom*, p. 50.
37. René Prieto, "A Semiotic Analysis of *Hombres de maíz* by Miguel Angel Asturias" (Ph.D. diss., Stanford University, 1980), p. 80.
38. *El libro del consejo*, pp. 182, 191.
39. Carmack, *The Quiché Mayas*, pp. 50, 203.

Notes for Chapter 4: Metamorphosis as Cosmic Refuge

1. The version consulted for this essay is Theodor Koch-Grünberg, "Mitos e Lendas dos Indios Taulipang e Arekuná," trans. Henrique Roenick, rev. M. Cavalcanti Proença.

2. In general the scholarship on *Macunaíma* is of very high quality. For another very fine structuralist study of *Macunaíma* the novel and *Macunaíma* the film, see John Randal Johnson, "Macunaíma: From Modernism to Cinema Novo" (Ph.D. diss., University of Texas, 1977). I would like to express here my appreciation to Randal Johnson both for reading and critiquing this chapter and for the loan of difficult-to-find materials.

3. Haroldo de Campos, *Morfologia do Macunaíma*, p. 58. The translation is my own.

4. Emir Rodríguez Monegal, "Anacronismos: Mário de Andrade y Guimarães Rosa en el contexto de la novela hispanoamericana," p. 112. The translation is my own.

5. Second preface to *Macunaíma*, written by Andrade in 1928, published in Telê Porto Ancona Lopez, *Macunaíma: A margem e o texto*, p. 92. The translation is my own.

6. First preface, written by Andrade in 1926, published in Lopez, *Margem*, p. 88 (translations of this work are my own).

7. For the full publishing history of *Macunaíma*, see the introduction to Mário de Andrade, *Macunaíma: O herói sem nenhum caráter*, edição crítica de Telê Porto Ancona Lopez (Rio de Janeiro: Livros Técnicos e Científicos Editora, 1978), pp. xv-lx. This edition, used in the preparation of this chapter, will be cited hereafter in the text as *Macunaíma*. There is no translation of *Macunaíma* available in English; however, I have consulted the excellent Spanish translation: *Macunaíma (El héroe sin ningún carácter)*, trans. Héctor Olea. All translations from the Portuguese in this chapter are my own.

8. Koch-Grünberg, "Mitos e Lendas," pp. 61–63.

9. Ibid., p. 63 (translations of this work are my own).

10. M. Cavalcanti Proença, *Roteiro de Macunaíma*, p. 170. This is the classic handbook for the study of *Macunaíma*; Proença's notes, commentary, and glossary are indispensable.

11. Proença, *Roteiro*, p. 172, explains that this distich comes from (1) the constant references by the chroniclers to the damage caused by the *saúva* ants to the farming endeavors of the colonists; (2) the famous phrase of Saint Hilaire: "Either Brazil must finish off the *saúva* or the *saúva* will finish Brazil"; and (3) another famous phrase by Professor Miguel Pereira: "Brazil is a vast hospital."

12. Lopez, *Margem*, p. 48.

13. The *jaboti* or *jabuti* is a Brazilian fruit-eating land turtle. In 1927 Andrade published a collection of poetry, *Clan do jaboti*, in which he represents the *jaboti* as the totem animal of Brazil.

14. M. M. Bakhtin, "Forms of Time and of the Chronotope in the Novel," in *The Dialogic Imagination: Four Essays by M. M. Bakhtin*, ed. and trans. Michael Holquist, p. 84. For an interesting Bakhtinian analysis of *Macunaíma*, see Mário Chamie, "Mário de Andrade: Fato Aberto e Discurso Carnavalesco," pp. 95–108. Chamie does not treat the concept of chronotope with regard to *Macunaíma*.

15. Isidore Ducasse, *Comte de Lautréamont: Oeuvres complètes*, ed. Philippe Soupault, p. 289.

16. Andrade makes the point, in his second preface, that Macunaíma is not even Brazilian (he is from an area in Venezuela) (Lopez, *Margem*, p. 91).

17. Proença, *Roteiro*, pp. 185–86.

18. Telê Porto Ancona Lopez, *Mário de Andrade: Ramais e caminho*, pp. 147–48.

19. Telê Lopez makes frequent reference to the fact that throughout Andrade's career, one of his major preoccupations was to "desgeograficar" Brazil.

No Prefácio, explica a quebra de límites de fauna, flora, personagens, como uma tentativa de globalizar o Brasil, de dar a síntese nacional exigida pela rapsódia. No romance exemplifica com a prática, criando um todo dinâmico de visualização do país e de interrogações baseadas mais nos elementos expostos, do que nas regiões de origem, se as tivesse conservado certas, ou mesmo declaradas. Fica a peculiaridade de um engenho açucareiro do Rio Grande do Norte, Bom Jardim, plantado no sul do país; peixes de tôdas as águas brasileiras habitam um mesmo local. As escapadas panorâmicas de Macunaíma dão bem a dimensão e a pluralidade de situações englobadas num todo brasileiro dinâmico, presente-passado, sem particularização geográfica. (Lopez, *Ramais*, 210)

(In the preface, he explains the breaking of the boundaries of fauna, flora, and characters, as an attempt to globalize Brazil, to give the national synthesis required by the rhapsody. In the novel he exemplifies in practice, creating a dynamic whole in the vision of the country and in the questions based more on the elements presented, than on the regions of origin, if he had kept them correct or even said what they were. We find the peculiarity of a sugar mill from Rio Grande do Norte, Bom Jardin, set in the southern part of the country; fish from all different Brazilian regions inhabit the same locale. The panoramic escapades of Macunaíma convey very well the dimension of the plurality of locations comprised in a dynamic Brazilian whole, present-past, without geographic particularization.) (my translation)

20. Lopez, *Ramais*, p. 105.
21. Koch-Grünberg, "Mitos e Lendas," p. 21.
22. Lopez, *Margem*, p. 18.
23. Oswald de Andrade, "Manifesto antropófago," in *Obras Completas*, vol. 6, 2d ed., ed. Benedito Nunes (Rio de Janeiro: Civilização Brasileira, 1972), p. 14. The translation is my own.
24. Lopez, *Margem*, pp. 18-19.
25. Count Hermann A. Keyserling, *The World in the Making*, trans. Maurice Samuel, p. 224.
26. Koch-Grünberg, "Mitos e Lendas," pp. 31-35.
27. Andrade was a Christian and a Catholic at least through the twenties, so that it is improbable that religious irony is intended in the characterization of Macunaíma.
28. Andrade, second preface, in Lopez, *Margem*, pp. 91-92.
29. According to Proença, *Roteiro*, p. 296, the *saci* is an entity from Indian mythology, sometimes evil, sometimes funny and jeering, represented by a small black man with one leg, a red stocking cap, and pipe; he makes himself known by a mysterious hissing, difficult to locate at night, and he amuses himself by frightening travelers and dispersing cattle herds from the ranches and horses from their pastures.
30. Lopez, *Ramais*, p. 168 (translations of this work are my own).
31. Lopez, *Ramais*, p. 198.
32. The "pai," or father, is the original ancestor of that species. See Proença, *Roteiro*, p. 286, or Koch-Grünberg, "Mitos e Lendas," pp. 35-36.
33. See Lopez, *Ramais*, pp. 126-36.
34. Lopez, *Ramais*, p. 127.
35. Mário de Andrade, from the manuscript of *Na pancada do ganzá*, a work never published, as quoted in Lopez, *Ramais*, p. 128.
36. Mário de Andrade, from the manuscript "Bumba-Introdução," as quoted in Lopez, *Ramais*, p. 131.
37. Andrade, "Bumba-Introdução," as quoted in Lopez, *Ramais*, p. 132.
38. For a wonderful example of a folk song that tells what each part of the ox's body will be used for, see Lopez, *Ramais*, pp. 134-35.
39. Lopez, *Ramais*, p. 187.
40. Mário de Andrade, "O castigo de ser," *Diário Nacional*, São Paulo (29 November 1931), as quoted in Lopez, *Ramais*, p. 237.
41. Campos, *Morfologia*, p. 147.
42. Angel Rama, "Mário de Andrade: Fundador de la nueva narrativa," pp. 31. The translation is my own.

Notes for Chapter 5: Metamorphosis as Creation Game

1. Johan Huizinga, *Homo Ludens: A Study of the Play Element in Culture*. This paragraph is a summary of the first chapter, "Nature and Significance of Play as a Cultural Phenomenon," pp. 19-46.
2. For other discussions of game in Cortázar's short fiction, see Jaime Alazraki, "Homo sapiens vs. homo ludens en tres cuentos de Julio Cortázar," *Revista Iberoamericana* 39 (1973): 611-24; and Linda Cummings Baxt, "Game in Cortázar" (Ph.D. diss., Yale University, 1974).
3. David Lagmanovich, "Prólogo: Para una caracterización general de los cuentos de Julio Cortázar," in *Estudios sobre los cuentos de Julio Cortázar*, ed. David Lagmanovich, pp. 11-13.

4. One of the principal studies of animals in Cortázar is Lucille Kerr, "The Beast and the Double: A Study of the Short Stories of Julio Cortázar" (Ph.D. diss., Yale University, 1972).

5. Julio Cortázar, *Bestiario*, 19th ed., p. 31, cited hereafter in the text as *Bestiario*. Translations of quoted passages are my own.

6. Doris Sommer, "Pattern and Predictability in the Stories of Julio Cortázar," in *The Contemporary Latin American Short Story*, ed. Rose S. Minc, pp. 71–81. On page 78, Sommer writes: "One cannot help imagining that Kafka's 'Metamorphosis' significantly informed this mode of Cortázar's narrative [a pattern of quantitative rather than qualitative change]. Once the almost unbelievable premise of a salesman turned cockroach is accepted, the rest follows with a ruthless and inevitable logic that traps the protagonist as well as the reader. Cortázar has learned to trap us, or more accurately, to illustrate that we are trapped in as masterful and often more subtle way." Although I agree with the comparison to Kafka, I would argue that Sommer's description of the pattern of predictability in Cortázar is oversimplified. As I have argued, the game does not always end in the same way, and "Axolotl," for one example, is in no way pessimistic.

7. Jaime Alazraki, "Introduction: Toward the Last Square of the Hopscotch," in *The Final Island: The Fiction of Julio Cortázar*, ed. Jaime Alazraki and Ivar Ivask, p. 10.

8. Julio Cortázar, "Axolotl," *Final del juego*, p. 123, cited hereafter in the text as "Axolotl." Translations are my own.

9. This point is made by Kerr, "The Beast," p. 74, and by Antonio Planells, "Comunicación por metamorfosis," pp. 135–41. My information comes from David Attenborough's television series "Life on Earth," which includes about a minute of footage of axolotls in their natural habitat and commentary placing them in the evolutionary scale and comparing them to salamanders. They are a grayish color in this footage.

10. Hernán Vidal interprets the longing to become the axolotl as the longing for death, in " 'Axolotl' y el deseo de morir," pp. 398–406.

11. Julio Cortázar, as quoted in Evelyn Picón Garfield, *Cortázar por Cortázar*, p. 55.

12. Cortázar denies the connection between "Para una poética" and "Axolotl," claiming that the man has left his consciousness behind in the animal and is now a walking zombie (Garfield, *Cortázar*, p. 55). Several lines from the text would seem to refute this. For one thing, the axolotl says clearly that what was the man's obsession is now an axolotl. Surely, even though an obsession may be considered to consume mind and soul for a time, it has at least temporal limitations and cannot be the totality of a being's consciousness. Furthermore, how could a zombie have the potential to write a story?

13. Ana María Hernández discusses Cortázar's poetics in terms of chameleonism, according to which the poet has no being of his own but is everything and nothing (the idea comes from Keats, whose influence on Cortázar is acknowledged and profound), and vampirism, according to which the poet must know but also *possess* the being of the Other (an attitude derived from Poe) ("Camaleonismo y vampirismo: La poética de Julio Cortázar," pp. 475–92).

14. Roman Ingarden, *The Literary Work of Art: An Investigation on the Borderlines of Ontology, Logic, and Theory of Literature*, trans. George G. Grabowicz, pp. 360–64.

15. After planning this chapter, I came across Antonio Pagés Larraya's fine article, "Perspectivas de 'Axolotl,' cuento de Julio Cortázar." Independently, we have arrived at the same conclusion: that the axolotl symbolizes the work of art. Nevertheless, our approaches and the implications we derive from the same finding are significantly different.

Notes for Chapter 6: Metamorphosis as Revenge

1. Luis Harss and Barbara Dohmann, *Into the Mainstream: Conversations with Latin American Writers*, p. 306.

2. Carlos Fuentes, *Zona sagrada*, p. 6, cited hereafter in the text as *Zona*. All translations are my own.

3. In an interview, Fuentes explained that the versions of the Ulysses myth recorded in *Zona*

Notes

sagrada come from Robert Graves' *Greek Myths*. See Emir Rodríguez Monegal, "Situación del escritor en América Latina," p. 15.

4. Gloria Durán, *La magia y las brujas en la obra de Carlos Fuentes*, p. 103. The translation is my own.

5. Antonio Caso, *La religión de los Aztecas*, pp. 45-46. The translation is my own.

6. Liliana Befumo Boschi and Elisa Calabrese, *Nostalgia del futuro en la obra de Carlos Fuentes*. Befumo Boschi and Calabrese also point out the link between Coatlicue and Tlazotéotl, another ancient earth goddess, devourer of filth. Fuentes links Claudia to Tlazotéotl as well. Befumo Boschi and Calabrese quote the following passage from *Zona sagrada*: "Tlazotéotl era la diosa indígena de la muerte, la fertilidad y la inmundicia: sus manos embarradas de sangre y excremento eran también las manos—bastaba despojarlas de los guantes ceremoniales—de la purificación: el que limpia se ensucia. La veo, confundida y segura, con un pie en el rito y otro en el juego" (Tlazotéotl was the Indian goddess of death, fertility and filth; her hands smeared with blood and excrement were also the hands—it is enough to strip them of their ceremonial gloves—of purification: the one who cleans gets herself dirty. I see her, confused and sure, with one foot in ritual and the other in the game) (*Zona*, 45).

7. For discussions of these three works as a trilogy, see Margaret Sayers Peden, "The World of the Second Reality in Three Novels by Carlos Fuentes," in *Otros mundos, otros fuegos; Fantasía y realismo mágico en Iberoamérica*, ed., Donald Yates, pp. 83-87; and Frank Dauster, "The Wounded Vision: *Aura, Zona sagrada*, and *Cumpleaños*," in *A Critical View: Carlos Fuentes*, ed. Robert Brody and Charles Rossman, pp. 106-20.

8. Carlos Fuentes, *Cumpleaños*, pp. 59-60. The translation is my own.

9. Dauster, "Wounded Vision," p. 113.

10. Lanín Gyurko, "The Sacred and the Profane in Fuentes' *Zona sagrada*," pp. 190-91.

11. See Durán's chapter, "*Zona sagrada* 'La bruja cabal,'" *La magia*, pp. 89-123.

12. Laurette Séjourné, *Burning Water: Thought and Religion in Ancient Mexico*, p. 70.

13. Ibid., p. 77.

14. Octavio Paz, *El laberinto de la soledad*, p. 72 (translations of this work are my own).

15. Ibid., pp. 76-77.

16. Andrés O. Avellaneda, "Mito y negación de la historia en *Zona sagrada* de Carlos Fuentes," pp. 247. The translation is my own.

Notes for Chapter 7: Conclusion

1. See Nancy Gray Díaz, "Metamorphosis from Human to Animal Form in Five Modern Latin American Narratives" (Ph.D. diss., Rutgers University, 1984).

2. M. M. Bakhtin, "Forms of Time and the Chronotope in the Novel: Notes Toward a Historical Poetics," *The Dialogic Imagination: Four Essays by M. M. Bakhtin*, ed. Michael Holquist and trans. Caryl Emerson and Michael Holquist, p. 112.

Bibliography

General Sources

Anderson Imbert, Enrique. *El realismo mágico y otros ensayos*. Caracas: Monte Avila, 1976.
Bleibtreu, John N. *The Parable of the Beast*. New York: Collier Books, 1968.
Carpentier, Alejo. *El reino de este mundo*. Mexico, D.F.: Edición y Distribución Iberoamericana de Publicaciones, 1949.
Cortázar, Julio. "Para una póetica." *La Torre* 2, vii (1954), pp. 121-38.
Dessau, Adalbert. "Realismo mágico y nueva novela latinoamericana: Consideraciones metodológicas e históricas." In *Actas del Simposio Internacional de Estudios Hispánicos*, ed. Horanyi Matyas, pp. 351-58. Budapest: Akad. Kiado, 1978.
Fergusson, Francis. Introductory essay to *Aristotle's Poetics*, trans. S. H. Butcher. New York: Hill and Wang, 1961.
Heidegger, Martin. *Being and Time*. Trans. John Macquarrie and Edward Robinson. New York: Harper & Row, 1962.
Husserl, Edmund. *Cartesian Meditations: An Introduction to Phenomenology*. Trans. Dorion Cairns. The Hague: Martinus Nijhoff, 1973.
Johnstone, Henry W., Jr. *The Problem of the Self.* University Park, Pa.: Pennsylvania State University Press, 1970.
Leal, Luis. "El realismo mágico en la literatura hispanoamericana." *Cuadernos Americanos* 153 (1967), pp. 230-35.
Lévi-Strauss, Claude. "L'Analyse morphologique des contes russes." *International Journal of Slavic Linguistics* 3 (1960), pp. 122-49.
López Alvarez, Luis. *Conversaciones con Miguel Angel Asturias*. Madrid: Editorial Magisterio Español, 1974.
Massey, Irving. *The Gaping Pig: Literature and Metamorphosis*. Berkeley: University of California Press, 1976.
Merleau-Ponty, M. *Phenomenology of Perception*. Trans. Colin Smith. New York: Humanities Press, 1962.
Nagel, Thomas. "What is it like to be a Bat?" *Philosophical Review* 83, no. 4 (October 1974), pp. 435-50.
Paz, Octavio. *Las peras del olmo*. Mexico, D.F.: Imprenta Universitaria, 1957.
Poulet, Georges. "Phenomenology of Reading." *New Literary History* 1, no. 1 (Fall 1969), pp. 53-68.
———. *Studies in Human Time*. Trans. Elliott Coleman. Baltimore: Johns Hopkins University Press, 1956.
Ricoeur, Paul. *Freedom and Nature: The Voluntary and the Involuntary*. Trans. Erazim V. Kohàk. Evanston: Northwestern University Press, 1966.
Skulsky, Harold. *Metamorphosis: The Mind in Exile*. Cambridge, Mass.: Harvard University Press, 1981.
Todorov, Tzvetan. *The Fantastic: A Structural Approach to a Literary Genre*. Trans. Richard Howard. Cleveland: Case Western Reserve University Press, 1973.

Wölfflin, Heinrich. *Principles of Art History: The Problem of the Development of Style in Later Art*. 6th ed. Trans. M. D. Hottinger. New York: Dover Publications, n.d.

Carpentier and *El reino de este mundo*

Carpentier, Alejo. *El acoso*. Barcelona: Bruguera, 1979.
——. *Cuentos completos*. 3d ed. Barcelona: Bruguera, 1979.
——. *Ecué-Yamba-O*. 3d. ed. Barcelona: Bruguera, 1979.
——. *The Kingdom of this World*. Trans. Harriet de Onís. New York: Alfred Knopf, 1957.
——. *Letra y solfa I: Visión de América*. Ed. Alexis Márquez Rodríguez. Buenos Aires: Lotus Mare, 1976.
——. *El reino de este mundo*. Mexico, D.F.: Edición y Distribución Iberoamericana de Publicaciones, 1949.
——. *El siglo de las luces*. 3d ed. Barcelona: Barral Editores, 1972.
——. *Tientos y diferencias*. Buenos Aires: Calicanto Editorial, 1976.
Arango L., Manuel A. "Correlación surrealista y social en dos novelas: *El reino de este mundo* de Alejo Carpentier y *Hombres de maíz* de Miguel Angel Asturias." *Explicación de Textos Literarios* 7 (1978), pp. 23–30.
Barrera, Ernesto M. "El vodú y el sacrificio del totem en *El reino de este mundo*." *Cuadernos Americanos* 211 (1977), pp. 148–57.
Benedetti, Mario. "Homenaje a Alejo Carpentier." *Cuadernos Americanos* 231 (1980), pp. 53–61.
Burgos Ojeda, Roberto. "La magia como elemento fundamental en la nueva narrativa latinoamericana." In *El ensayo en la crítica literaria en Iberoamérica: Memoria del XIV Congreso del Instituto Internacional de Literatura Iberoamericana*, ed. Kurt L. Levy and Keith Ellis. Toronto: University of Toronto Press, 1970.
Celorio, Gonzalo. *El surrealismo y lo real maravilloso americano*. Mexico, D.F.: Secretaría de Educación Pública, 1976.
Cheuse, Alan. "Memories of the Future: A Critical Biography of Alejo Carpentier." Ph.D. diss., Rutgers University, 1974.
Cvitanovic, Dinko. "Lo barroco, clave de confluencias en la obra narrativa de Alejo Carpentier." *Revista/Review Interamericana* 4 (1974), pp. 370–84.
Durán Luzio, Juan. "Nuestra América, el gran propósito de Alejo Carpentier." *Cuadernos Americanos* 233 (1980), pp. 22–34.
Faris, Wendy B. "Alejo Carpentier à la recherche du temps perdu." *Comparative Literature Studies* 17 (1980), pp. 133–54.
Giacoman, Helmy F., ed. *Homenaje a Alejo Carpentier: Variaciones interpretativas en torno a su obra*. New York: Las Américas, 1970.
González Echevarría, Roberto. *Alejo Carpentier: The Pilgrim at Home*. Ithaca, N.Y.: Cornell University Press, 1977.
——. "Historia y alegoría en la narrativa de Carpentier." *Cuadernos Americanos* 228 (1980), pp. 200–220.
Irish, James. "Magical Realism: A Search for Caribbean and Latin American Roots." *Revista/Review Interamericana* 4 (1974), pp. 411–21.
Jitrik, Noé. "Blanco, Negro, Mulato? Una lectura de *El reino de este mundo* de Alejo Carpentier." *Texto Crítico* 1 (1975), pp. 32–60.
Lamb, Ruth S. "El exuberante barroquismo de Alejo Carpentier." In *XVII Congreso*

del Instituto Internacional de Literatura Iberoamericana: El barroco en América; Literatura hispanoamericana; Crítica histórico-literaria hispanoamericana, pp. 489–98. Madrid: Cultura Hispánica, 1980.

Leal, Luis. "Magical Realism in Spanish American Fiction." *Hispania* 38, no. 2 (1955), pp. 187–92.

Macdonald, Ian R. "Magical Eclecticism: *Los pasos perdidos* and Jean-Paul Sartre." *Forum for Modern Language Studies* 15 (1979), pp. 97–113.

Márquez Rodríguez, Alexis. *La obra narrativa de Alejo Carpentier*. Caracas: Edición de la Biblioteca, Universidad Central de Venezuela, 1970.

Mazziotti, Nora, ed. *Historia y mito en la obra de Alejo Carpentier*. Buenos Aires: Fernando García Cambeiro, 1972.

Mena, Lucila-Inés. "Hacia una formulación teórica del realismo mágico." *Bulletin Hispanique* 77 (1975), pp. 395–407.

Menton, Seymour. "Lo nuevo y lo viejo en el nuevo neobarroco de Alejo Carpentier." In *XVII Congreso del Instituto Internacional de Literatura Iberoamericana: El barroco en América; Literatura hispanoamericana; Crítica histórico-literaria hispanoamericana*, pp. 481–87. Madrid: Cultura Hispánica, 1980.

Merrell, Floyd. "The Ideal World in Search of its Reference: An Inquiry into the Underlying Nature of Magical Realism." *Chasqui* 4 (1975), pp. 5–17.

Métraux, Alfred. *Le Vaudou haïtien*. Paris: Gallimard, 1958.

Mocega-González, Esther P. "*El reino de este mundo* de Alejo Carpentier." *Cuadernos Hispanoamericanos* 222–223 (1977), pp. 219–39.

Müller-Bergh, Klaus. *Alejo Carpentier: Estudio biográfico-crítico*. New York: Las Américas, 1972.

Müller-Bergh, et al. *Asedios a Carpentier: Once ensayos críticos sobre el novelista cubano*. Santiago de Chile: Editorial Universitaria, 1972.

Oleriny, Vladimir. "Le 'Réalisme Magique' d'Alejo Carpentier." *Philogica Pragensia* 23 (1980), pp. 112–13.

Pickenhayn, Jorge Oscar. *Para leer a Alejo Carpentier*. Buenos Aires: Plus Ultra, 1978.

Quesada, Luis. "Desarrollo evolutivo del elemento negro en tres de las primeras narraciones de Alejo Carpentier." In *Novela Iberoamericana Contemporánea*, vol. 3, pp. 217–23. Lima: Cuadernos de Literatura de la Emancipación Hispanoamericana y Otros Ensayos, 1971.

Rodríguez, Ileana. "En busca de una expresión antillana: Lo real maravilloso en Carpentier y Alexis." *Ideology and Literature* 2 (1979), pp. 56–68.

Sánchez-Boudy, José. *La temática novelística de Alejo Carpentier*. Miami: Ediciones Universitarias, 1969.

Speratti-Piñero, Emma Susana. "Noviciado y apoteosis de Ti Noel en 'El reino de este mundo.'" *Bulletin Hispanique* 80 (1978), pp. 201–28.

Valbuena Briones, Angel. "Una cala en el realismo mágico." *Cuadernos Americanos* 166 (1969), pp. 233–41.

Yates, Donald A., ed. *Otros mundos, otros fuegos: Fantasía y realismo mágico*. East Lansing, Mich.: Latin American Studies Center of Michigan State University, 1975.

Miguel Angel Asturias and *Hombres de maíz*

Asturias, Miguel Angel. *América, Fábula de fábulas y otros ensayos*. Ed. Richard Callan. Caracas: Monte Avila, 1972.

———. *Hombres de maíz*. Buenos Aires: Editorial Losada, 1949.
———. *Leyendas de Guatemala*. 5th ed. Buenos Aires: Editorial Losada, 1957.
———. *Men of Maize*. Trans. Gerald Martin. New York: Delacorte Press, 1975.
———. *Mulata de tal*. Buenos Aires: Editorial Losada, 1963.
Bellini, Giuseppe. *La narrativa de Miguel Angel Asturias*. Trans. Ignacio Soriano. Buenos Aires: Editorial Losada, 1969.
Bernu, Michéle. "Mythe et société dans *Hombres de maíz* de Miguel Angel Asturias." *Cahiers de Monde Hispanique et Luso-Brésilien* 24 (1977), pp. 45–64.
Brinton, Daniel G. *Nagualism: A Study in Native American Folk-lore and History*. Philadelphia: McCalla & Co., 1894.
Brotherston, Gordon. "The Presence of Mayan Literature in *Hombres de maíz* and other Works by Miguel Angel Asturias." *Hispania* 58 (1975), pp. 68–74.
Callan, Richard J. "The Quest Myth in Miguel Angel Asturias' *Hombres de maíz*," *Hispanic Review* 36 (1968), pp. 249–61.
Carmack, Robert M. *The Quiché Mayas of Utatlán: The Evolution of a Highland Guatemalan Kingdom*. Norman: University of Oklahoma Press, 1981.
Carreño, Antonio. "Lenguaje y formas estilísticas en *El señor presidente* y *Hombres de maíz* de Miguel Angel Asturias." *Cuadernos Americanos* 136 (1973), pp. 231–41.
Castelpoggi, Atilio Jorge. *Miguel Angel Asturias*. Buenos Aires: Editorial "La Mandragora," 1961.
Corvalán, Octavio. "*Hombres de maíz*: Una novela-mito." *Journal of Spanish Studies: Twentieth Century* 7 (1979), pp. 33–40.
García, Emilio F. *Hombres de maíz: Unidad y sentido a través de sus símbolos mitológicos*. Miami: Ediciones Universal, 1978.
Giacoman, Helmy F. *Homenaje a Miguel Angel Asturias*. New York: Las Américas, 1971.
Girard, Raphael. *Esotericism of the Popol Vuh*. Trans. Blair A. Moffett. Pasadena: Theosophical University Press, 1979.
Guibert, Rita. *Seven Voices: Seven Latin American Writers Talk to Rita Guibert*. Trans. Frances Partridge. New York: Vintage Books, 1972.
Harss, Luis, and Barbara Dohmann. *Into the Mainstream: Conversations with Latin American Writers*. New York: Harper & Row, 1967.
Kaplan, Lucille N. "*Tonal* and *Nagual* in Coastal Oaxaca Mexico." *Journal of American Folklore* 69 (1956), pp. 363–68.
El libro del consejo. 3d ed. Trans. Georges Raynaud, J. M. González de Mendoza, and Miguel Angel Asturias. Mexico, D.F.: UNAM, 1964.
Lorand de Olazagasti, Adelaida. *El indio en la narrativa guatemalteca*. San Juan, Puerto Rico: Editorial Universitaria, 1968.
Martin, G. M. "Pattern for a Novel: Analysis of the Opening of *Hombres de maíz*." *Revista de Estudios Hispánicos* 5 (1971), pp. 223–41.
———. "Theme and Structure in Asturias' *Hombres de maíz*." *Modern Language Quarterly* 30 (1969), pp. 582–602.
Meneses, Miguel. *Miguel Angel Asturias*. Madrid: Ediciones Jucar, 1975.
Menton, Seymour. *Historia crítica de la novela guatemalteca*. Guatemala: Editorial Universitaria, 1960.
Pitt-Rivers, Julian. "Spiritual Power in Central America: The Naguals of Chiapas." In *Witchcraft Confessions and Accusations*, ed. Mary Douglas, pp. 183–206. London: Tavistock Publications, 1970.

Popol Vuh: The Sacred Book of the Ancient Quiché Maya. Trans. Delia Goetz and Sylvanus G. Morley. Norman: University of Oklahoma Press, 1950.
Popov Maligec, Vera. "Telluric Forces and Literary Creativity in Miguel Angel Asturias." Ph.D. diss., Columbia University, 1976.
Prieto, René. "A Semiotic Analysis of *Hombres de maíz* by Miguel Angel Asturias." Ph.D. diss., Stanford University, 1980.
Rozzotto, Jaime Díaz. "El *Popol Vuh*: Fuente estética del realismo mágico de Miguel Angel Asturias." *Cuadernos Americanos* 201 (1975), pp. 85–92.
Saenz, Jimena. *Genio y figura de Miguel Angel Asturias*. Buenos Aires: Editorial Universitaria de Buenos Aires, 1974.
Saler, Benson. *Nagual, brujo y hechicero en un pueblo quiché*. Guatemala: Editorial José Pineda Ibarra, 1964.
Spitzer, Leo. *Linguistics and Literary History: Essays in Stylistics*. Princeton, N.J.: Princeton University Press, 1948.

Mário de Andrade and *Macunaíma*

Andrade, Mário de. *Amar, verbo intransitivo: Idílio*. São Paulo: Livraria Martins Editora, n.d.
———. *Aspectos da literatura brasileira*. 5th ed. São Paulo: Livraria Martins Editora, 1974.
———. *Cartas a Manuel Bandeira*. Rio de Janeiro: Organização Simões, 1958.
———. *Macunaíma (El héroe sin ningún carácter)*. Trans. Héctor Olea. Barcelona: Editorial Seix Barral, 1977.
———. *Macunaíma: O herói sem nenhum caráter*. Ed. Telê Porto Ancona Lopez. Rio de Janeiro: Livros Técnicos e Científicos Editora, 1978.
———. *O movimento modernista*. Rio de Janeiro: Casa do Estudante, 1942.
———. *Poesias completas*, 6th ed. São Paulo: Livraria Martins Editora, 1980.
Andrade, Oswald de. "Manifesto antropófago." In *Obras completas*, vol. 6, 2d. ed., ed. Benedito Nunes. Rio de Janeiro: Civilização Brasileira, 1970.
Bakhtin, M. M. *The Dialogic Imagination: Four Essays by M. M. Bakhtin*. Ed. Michael Holquist. Trans. Caryl Emerson and Michael Holquist. Austin: University of Texas Press, 1981.
Campos, Haroldo de. *Morfologia do Macunaíma*. São Paulo: Editora Perspectiva, 1973.
Chamie, Mário. *Intertexto: A escrita rapsódica—ensaio de leitura produtora*. São Paulo: Edição Praxis, 1970.
———. "Mário de Andrade: Fato Aberto e Discurso Carnavalesco." *Revista Iberoamericana* 43 (1977), pp. 95–108.
Dole, Gertrude, Dale W. Kietzman, et al. *Indians of Brazil in the Twentieth Century*. Ed. Janice H. Hopper. Washington, D.C.: Institute for Cross-Cultural Research, 1967.
Ducasse, Isidore. *Comte de Lautréamont: Oeuvres complètes*. Ed. Philippe Soupault. Paris: Charlot, 1946.
Frazer, Sir James George. *The Golden Bough; A Study in Magic and Religion*, vol 1. New York: Macmillan, 1950.
Freud, Sigmund. *Totem and Taboo: Some Points of Agreement between the Mental Lives of Savages and Neurotics*. Trans. James Strachey. New York: W. W. Norton, 1950.

Johnson, John Randal. "*Macunaíma*: From Modernism to Cinema Novo." Ph.D. diss., University of Texas, 1973.
Keyserling, Count Hermann A. *The World in the Making*. Trans. Maurice Samuel. London: Jonathan Cape, 1927.
Koch-Grünberg, Theodor. "Mitos e Lendas dos Indios Taulipang e Arekuná." Trans. Henrique Roenick. Rev. M. Cavalcanti Proença. *Revista do Museu Paulista* 7 (1953), pp. 119–53.
Lima, Medeiros. "Mário de Andrade: O descobridor de um continente desconhecido." *Opinião* 7 (July 1975), pp. 9–10.
Lopez, Telê Porto Ancona. *Macunaíma: A margem e o texto*. São Paulo: HUCITEC, 1974.
———. *Mário de Andrade: Ramais e caminho*. São Paulo: Livraria Duas Cidades, 1972.
Loureiro Chaves, Flavio, et al. *Aspectos de modernismo brasileiro*. Porto Alegre: Universidade Federal do Rio Grande do Sul, 1970.
Martins, Wilson. *The Modernist Idea: A Critical Survey of Brazilian Writing in the Twentieth Century*. Trans. Jack E. Tomlins. New York: New York University Press, 1970.
Nist, John. *The Modernist Movement in Brazil: A Literary Study*. Austin: University of Texas Press, 1967.
Proença, M. Cavalcanti. *Roteiro de Macunaíma*. 5th ed. Rio de Janeiro: Civilização Brasileira, 1978.
Rabassa, Gregory. "A Comparative Look at the Literatures of Spanish America and Brazil: The Dangers of Deception." *Proceedings of the Comparative Literature Symposium* 10 (1978), pp. 119–32.
Rama, Angel. "Mário de Andrade: Fundador de la nueva narrativa." *Diálogos* 66 (1975), pp. 28–31.
Rodríguez Monegal, Emir. "Anacronismos: Mário de Andrade y Guimarães Rosa en el contexto de la novela hispanoamericana." *Revista Iberoamericana* 43 (1977), pp. 109–15.
Schnaiderman, Boris. "*Macunaíma*: un diálogo entre surdos." *O Estado de São Paulo Suplemento Literario* 27 (October 1974).

Julio Cortázar and "Axolotl"

Cortázar, Julio. *Bestiario*. 19th ed. Buenos Aires: Editorial Sudamericana, 1978.
———. *Final del juego*. 1st ed. Mexico, D.F.: Los Presentes, 1956.
———. "Para una poética." *La Torre* 2, vii (1954), pp. 121–38.
———. *Rayuela*. 6th ed. Buenos Aires: Editorial Sudamericana, 1968.
Alazraki, Jaime, and Ivar Ivask, eds. *The Final Island: The Fiction of Julio Cortázar*. Norman: University of Oklahoma Press, 1976.
Barrenechea, Ana María, and Emma Susana Speratti-Piñero. *La literatura fantástica en Argentina*. Mexico, D.F.: Imprenta Universitaria, 1957.
Baxt, Linda Cummings. "Game in Cortázar." Ph.D. diss., Yale University, 1974.
De la Fuente, Albert. "Tigres y estilos en 'Bestiario.'" *Explicación de Textos Literarios* 8 (1979–80), pp. 137–43.
Giacoman, Helmy F., ed. *Homenaje a Julio Cortázar: Variaciones interpretivas en torno a su obra*. Long Island City: Las Américas, 1972.

Hernández, Ana María. "Camaleonismo y vampirismo: La poética de Julio Cortázar." *Revista Iberoamericana* 45, cviii-ix (1979), pp. 475–92.
Hernández del Castillo, Ana. *Keats, Poe and the Shaping of Cortázar's Mythopoesis*. Amsterdam: John Benjamins B. V., 1981.
Huizinga, Johan. *Homo Ludens: A Study of the Play Element in Culture*. New York: Harper & Row, 1970.
Ingarden, Roman. *The Literary Work of Art: An Investigation on the Borderlines of Ontology, Logic, and Theory of Literature*. Trans. George G. Grabowicz. Evanston: Northwestern University Press, 1973.
Jitrik, Noé, Manuel Durand, et al. *La vuelta a Cortázar en nueve ensayos*. Buenos Aires: Carlos Pérez Editor, 1968.
Kerr, Lucille. "The Beast and the Double: A Study of the Short Stories of Julio Cortázar." Ph.D. diss., Yale University, 1972.
Lagmanovich, David, ed. *Estudios sobre los cuentos de Julio Cortázar*. Barcelona: Ediciones Hispam, 1975.
Mac Adam, Alfred. *El individuo y el otro: Crítica a los cuentos de Julio Cortázar*. Buenos Aires: Ediciones La Librería, 1971.
Mimoso-Ruiz, Duarte-Nuno. "*Circé* de Julio Cortázar." *Revue de Littérature Comparée* 52 (1978), pp. 60–73.
Minc, Rose S., ed. *The Contemporary Latin American Short Story*. New York: Senda Nueva de Ediciones, 1979.
Pagés Larraya, Antonio. "Perspectivas de 'Axolotl,' cuento de Julio Cortázar." *Nueva Narrativa Hispanoamericana* 2 (1972), pp. 7–24.
Picón Garfield, Evelyn. *Cortázar por Cortázar*. Mexico, D.F.: Centro de Investigaciones Linguístico-Literarias Universidad Veracruzana, 1978.
Planells, Antonio. "Comunicación por metamorfosis: 'Axolotl' de Julio Cortázar." *Explicación de Textos Literarios* 6, ii (1978), pp. 135–41.
―――. *Cortázar: Metafísica y erotismo*. Madrid: Studia Humanitatis, 1979.
Rein, Mercedes. *Cortázar y Carpentier*. Buenos Aires: Ediciones Crisis, 1974.
Sommer, Doris. "Playing to Lose: Cortázar's Comforting Pessimism." *Chasqui* 8, iii (May 1979), pp. 54–62.
Vidal, Hernán. "'Axolotl' y el deseo de morir." *Cuadernos Hispanoamericanos* 364–68 (1980–81), pp. 398–406.
Whittingham, Georgina. "The Bestiario by Cortázar: An Analysis of Traditional and Contemporary Themes." Master's thesis, Stanford University, 1972.

Carlos Fuentes and *Zona sagrada*

Fuentes, Carlos. *Cumpleaños*. 6th ed. Mexico D.F.: Editorial Joaquín Mortiz, 1969.
―――. "La nueva novela latinoamericana." In *La novela hispanoamericana*, 4th ed., ed. Juan Loveluck, pp. 164–94. Santiago, Chile: Editorial Universitaria, 1969.
―――. *Tiempo mexicano*. Mexico D.F.: Cuadernos de Joaquín Mortiz, 1972.
―――. *Zona sagrada*. Mexico D.F.: Siglo Veintiuno Editores, 1967.
Alba-Buffil, Elio. "En torno a *Zona sagrada* de Carlos Fuentes." In *Actas del Séptimo Congreso de la Asociación Internacional de Hispanistas*, vol. 1, ed. Giuseppe Bellini, pp. 175–82. Rome: Bulzoni Editori, 1982.

Avellaneda, Andrés O. "Mito y negación de la historia en *Zona sagrada* de Carlos Fuentes." *Cuadernos Americanos* 175 (1971), pp. 239–48.

Befumo Boschi, Liliana, and Elisa Calabrese. *Nostalgia del futuro en la obra de Carlos Fuentes*. Buenos Aires: Fernando García Cambeiro, 1974.

Brody, Robert, and Charles Rossman, eds. *A Critical View: Carlos Fuentes*. Austin: University of Texas Press, 1982.

Caso, Antonio. *La religión de los aztecas*. Mexico D.F.: Secretaría de Educación Pública, 1945.

Durán, Gloria. *La magia y las brujas en la obra de Carlos Fuentes*. Mexico, D.F.: Universidad Nacional Autónoma de México, 1976.

Giacoman, Helmy F., ed. *Homenaje a Carlos Fuentes: Variaciones interpretativas en torno a su obra*. New York: Las Américas, 1971.

Graves, Robert. *The Greek Myths*. Baltimore: Penguin, 1955.

Gyurko, Lanín. "The Myths of Ulysses in Fuentes's 'Zona sagrada.'" *Modern Language Review* 69 (1974), pp. 316–24.

―――. "The Pseudo-Liberated Woman in Fuentes' *Zona sagrada*." *Journal of Spanish Studies: Twentieth Century* 3 (1975), pp. 17–43.

―――. "The Sacred and the Profane in Fuentes' *Zona sagrada*." *Revista Hispánica Moderna* 37 (1972–1973), pp. 188–209.

Hagen, Victor Wolfgang von. *The Aztec: Man and Tribe*. Rev. ed. New York: Signet, 1961.

Hall, Linda B. "The Cipactli Monster: Woman as Destroyer in Carlos Fuentes." *Southwest Review* 60 (1975), pp. 246–55.

Krickeberg, Walter. *Mitos y leyendas de los aztecas, incas, mayas, muiscas*. Mexico, D.F.: Fondo de Cultura Económica, 1971.

Paz, Octavio. *El laberinto de la soledad*. 2d ed. Mexico D.F.: Fondo de Cultura Económica, 1959.

Rodríguez Monegal, Emir. "Situación del escritor en América Latina." *Mundo Nuevo* 1 (July 1966), pp. 5–21.

Sarduy, Severo. "Un fetiche de cachemira gris perla." In *Escrito sobre un cuerpo: Ensayos de crítica*, pp. 31–42. Buenos Aires: Editorial Sudamericana, 1969.

Sayers Peden, Margaret. "The World of the Second Reality in Three Novels by Carlos Fuentes." In *Otros mundos, otros fuegos: Fantasía y realismo mágico en Iberoamérica*, ed. Donald Yates, pp. 83–87. East Lansing, Mich.: Latin American Studies Center of Michigan State University, 1975.

Séjourné, Laurette. *Burning Water: Thought and Religion in Ancient Mexico*. Berkeley: Shambhala, 1976.

World Literature Today: A Literary Quarterly of the University of Oklahoma (Carlos Fuentes Issue) 57 (August 1983).

Index

Andrade, Mário de, 2, 12, 51–71. *See also Macunaíma*
Andrade, Oswald de (Brazilian Modernist, author of "Manifesto antropófago"), 60–61
Apuleius (author of *The Golden Ass*): aspects of metamorphosis in, 5, 101. *See also The Golden Ass*
Asturias, Miguel Angel, 34–50; as Magic Realist, 2; poetic theory of, 14. *See also Cuculcán, serpiente envuelta en plumas; Hombres de maíz; Leyendas de Guatemala; Mulata de tal*
"Axolotl," 2, 15, 72–82; body in, 76–77; game in, 71–72, 82; metamorphic crisis in, 47–50; mutability in, 72–76; perception in, 78–79; self in, 76–79; time in, 79–80; will in, 79. *See also* Julio Cortázar

Baroque style: aesthetic principles of, 4–5, 99; in *El reino de este mundo*, 24–26; in *Hombres de maíz*, 41; in Latin American art; in *Zona sagrada*, 86–88, 92, 96. *See also* Mutability
"Bestiario" (short story by Julio Cortázar), 74–75
Bestiario (collection of short stories by Julio Cortázar), 73–76
Body: concept of and effects of metamorphosis on, 7; in "Axolotl," 76–77; in *El reino de este mundo*, 30; in *Hombres de maíz*, 44–45; in *Macunaíma*, 64; in *Zona sagrada*, 90
Borges, Jorge Luis: compared to Magic Realists, 103n3

Carpentier, Alejo, 11–14, 16–33; compared to Asturias, 34; as Magic Realist, 2; mentioned, 64; theory of "lo real maravilloso," 2, 13–14. *See also* Baroque; *El reino de este mundo*; "Los fugitivos"; *Lo real maravilloso*; Magic Realism; *El siglo de las luces*
"Carta a una señorita en París" (short story by Julio Cortázar), 73–74
Chants de Maldoror (by Isidore Ducasse, Comte de Lautréamont), 58

Coatlicue (Aztec goddess): characterized, 85; in *Zona sagrada*, 84–85, 94–96
Cortázar, Julio, 2, 12, 72–82; poetic theory of, 14–15. *See also* "Axolotl"; *Bestiario*; "Carta a una señorita en París"; *Final del juego*; "Para una poética"; "Todos los fuegos el fuego"
Cuculcán, serpiente envuelta en plumas (play by Miguel Angel Asturias), 37
Cumpleaños (novel by Carlos Fuentes), 90

Doctor Faustus (novel by Thomas Mann), 50
Don Quijote (novel by Miguel de Cervantes), 40, 42, 99
Dostoevsky, Fyodor, 6
Double, The (novella by Fyodor Dostoevsky), 6
Doubling: as literary device for exploring contradictions in self, 6
Ducasse, Isidore (Comte de Lautréamont), 101

Euripidean soliloquy: as literary device for exploring contradictions in self, 6

Final del juego (collection of short stories by Julio Cortázar), 72, 76
Folk legend: in *Macunaíma*, 52–55, 62
Form: idea of, 1, 98
Fuentes Carlos, 2, 12, 83–97. *See also Cumpleaños; Zona sagrada*

Game: in "Axolotl," 71–72, 82; in *Zona sagrada*, 71, 83–84, 96–97
Golden Ass, The (work by Apuleius), 8
Golden Bough, The (by Sir James George Frazer), 67
Gregor Samsa (character in Franz Kafka's *The Metamorphosis*), 5, 7–8, 46, 75–76, 81, 92. *See also* Kafka, Franz; *The Metamorphosis*

Heidegger, Martin: concept of the "moment of vision," 29, 107n20; definition of Dasein, 3–4, 104n13; theory of Being-in-the-World, 64
History (as subject): in *El reino de este*

mundo, 18–19; in Latin American narrative, 2, 13–14; in *Zona sagrada*, 97
Hombres de maíz, 34–50; Baroque style in, 41; body in, 44–45; compared to *Zona sagrada*, 90; mentioned, 2; metamorphic crisis in, 100–101; mutability in, 34–42; myth in, 51; nagualism in, 45–46; perception in, 46; self in, 11; time in, 46–47; will in, 46. *See also* Asturias, Miguel Angel; *Popol Vuh*
Huizinga, Johan: theory of game, 72
Husserl, Edmund: theory of consciousness, 104n13

Ingarden, Roman: theory of intentional objectivity, 104n12; theory of ontology of work of art, 81–82
Intentional object: literary image as, 3

Johnstone, Henry: definition of "self," 6, 63

Kafka, Franz: aspects of metamorphosis in, 5, 7–8, 93, 101; compared to Mário de Andrade, 70; compared to Latin American Magic Realists, 103n3. *See also* Gregor Samsa; *The Metamorphosis*
Keyserling, Count Hermann (author of *The World in the Making*), 61–65
Koch-Grünberg, Theodor (ethnographer and author of *Vom Roroima zum Orinoco*), 51, 59, 62

Lévi-Strauss, Claude, 4
Leyendas de Guatemala (by Miguel Angel Asturias), 36
Lo real maravilloso, 2, 12–14. *See also* Carpentier, Alejo; *El reino de este mundo*; Magic Realism
"Los fugitivos" (story by Alejo Carpentier), 16–18, 30–31

Macunaíma, 2, 51–71, 102; body in, 64; metamorphic crisis in, 66–70; mutability in, 55–62; myth in, 51; perception in, 64–65; self in, 52, 63–64, 70; time in, 62, 66; will in, 65–66; as satire, 51, 70–71. *See also* Andrade, Mário de
Magic Realism, 2, 10–15, 99, 101–2, 103n3, 103n4, 103n6. *See also* Asturias, Miguel Angel; Carpentier, Alejo; *Lo real maravilloso*
Matriarchy: in *Hombres de maíz*, 70; in *Macunaíma*, 70

Merleau-Ponty, Maurice: theory of body, 104n21; theory of phenomenology, 103n11
Metamorphic crisis: concept of, 1, 9–10, 100–101; in "Axolotl," 80–82; in *El reino de este mundo*, 31–33; in *Hombres de maíz*, 47–50; in *Macunaíma*, 66–70; in *Zona sagrada*, 94–97
Metamorphosis, The (novella by Franz Kafka), 8, 75–76; compared to "Axolotl," 112n6. *See also* Gregor Samsa; Kafka, Franz
Mind: concept of, 1; mind/body dualism, 1, 5–6
Mulata de tal (novel by Miguel Angel Asturias), 37, 107n8
Mutability: concept of, 3–5, 98–100; in "Axolotl," 72–76; in *El reino de este mundo*, 18–26; in *Hombres de maíz*, 34–42; in *Macunaíma*, 55–62; in *Zona sagrada*, 86–90. *See also* Baroque; Narrative world
Myth: in *El reino de este mundo*, 71, 97; in *Hombres de maíz*, 52, 71; in *Macunaíma*, 52; in *Zona sagrada*, 83–85, 96–97. *See also* Coatlicue; Folk legend; Koch-Grünberg, Theodor; *Popol Vuh*; Quetzalcóatl; Voodoo; Xólotl

Nagualism: definitions of, 42; in *Hombres de maíz*, 42, 45–46
Narrative world, 1, 3–5, 98–99. *See also* Mutability
Neo-Baroque: as aspect of modern Latin American writing, 12. *See also* Baroque

Ovid: aspects of metamorphosis in, 6, 8, 101; his *The Metamorphoses* compared to *Zona sagrada*, 93; types of metamorphoses in, 5

"Para una poética" (essay by Julio Cortázar), 14–15, 80–81, 112n12. *See also* Cortázar, Julio
Paz, Octavio: on Mexican deities, 95–96; theory of magical art, 2, 10–11, 14
Perception: concept of and effects of metamorphosis on, 7–8; in "Axolotl," 78–79; in *El reino de este mundo*, 30–31; in *Hombres de maíz*, 46; in *Macunaíma*, 64–65; in *Zona sagrada*, 91
Phenomenology: as basis for literary investigation, 2–3, 15, 98
Poetics, The (of Aristotle), 9

Index

Popol Vuh, 34, 36-37, 41-42, 47-49, 101, 107n6, 108-9n26-27, 109n35
Poulet, Georges: phenomenology of reading, 11; on time, 9

Quetzalcóatl (Aztec god), 85, 94-95

Reino de este mundo, El, 11-14, 16-33; Baroque style in, 24-26; body in, 30; compared to *Hombres de maíz*, 42-43, 50; history in, 97; mentioned, 2, 66; metamorphic crisis in, 31-33; mutability in, 99; myth in, 34, 51, 97; perception in, 27, 30-31; self in, 11; time in, 99; will in, 31. *See also* Carpentier, Alejo; *Lo real maravilloso*; Magic Realism
Revista de Antropofagia (journal of Brazilian Modernism), 61
Ricoeur, Paul: on mind/body dualism, 5-6; on will, 8-9, 16-17, 104n23-24

Satire: in *Macunaíma*, 52-55, 70-71
Self: concept of and effects of metamorphosis on, 1, 3-4, 5-6, 10-11, 100; literary techniques for exploring, 6; in "Axolotl," 76-79; in *El reino de este mundo*, 30; in *Hombres de maíz*, 45-46; in *Macunaíma*, 52, 63-64, 70, in *Zona sagrada*, 91

Siglo de las luces, El (novel by Alejo Carpentier), 24-25

Time: concept of and effects of metamorphosis on, 9; in "Axolotl," 79-80; in *El reino de este mundo*, 19-20, 31, 33; in *Hombres de maíz*, 46-47; in *Macunaíma*, 62, 66; in *Zona sagrada*, 91-93, 97
"Todos los fuegos el fuego" (short story by Julio Cortázar), 79
Totem and Taboo (by Sigmund Freud), 59

Voodoo, 23-24, 28, 105n6, 105-6n10, 106n12, 106-7n18

Will: concept of and effects of metamorphosis on, 8-9; in "Axolotl," 79; in *El reino de este mundo*, 31; in *Hombres de maíz*, 46; in *Macunaíma*, 65-66; in *Zona sagrada*, 91-93
Wölfflin, Heinrich: on Baroque art, 4

Xólotl (Axtec god), 85, 94-95

Zona sagrada, 2, 83-97, 100; Baroque style in, 86-88, 92, 96; body in, 90; compared to "Axolotl," 79; game in, 71, 83-84, 96-97; history in, 97; metamorphic crisis in, 94-97; mutability in, 86-90; myth in, 83-85, 96-97; perception in, 91; self in, 91; time in, 91-93, 97; will in, 91-93. *See also* Fuentes, Carlos